Stories on Stage

Scripts for Reader's Theater

Stories on Stage

Scripts for
Reader's Theater

Aaron Shepard

The H. W. Wilson Company
1993

Printed in the United States of America
First Printing

Library of Congress Cataloging-in-Publication Data

Stories on stage: scripts for reader's theater /
[edited] by Aaron Shepard.
p.   cm.
Includes bibliographical references and index.
Summary: A collection of twenty-two plays adapted from folk tales, short stories, myths, and novels and intended for use in reader's theater programs with middle grade and junior high school students.
ISBN 0-8242-0851-X
1. Children's plays. American.   2. Reader's theater.   [1. Plays.
2. Reader's theater.]   I. Shepard, Aaron.
PS625.5.S76   1993
812'.540809282—dc20   91-42236

Acknowledgments

The author is grateful for permission to adapt and include the following works:

"The Bean Boy," from *California Fairy Tales*, by Monica Shannon. Copyright © 1926 by Doubleday, a division of Bantam Doubleday Dell Publishing Group, Inc. Used by permission of Doubleday, a division of Bantam Doubleday Dell Publishing Group, Inc.

The Devil and Mother Crump, by Valerie Scho Carey. Text copyright © 1987 by Valerie Scho Carey. Selection reprinted by permission of HarperCollins Publishers.

The Feather Merchants, and Other Tales of the Fools of Chelm, by Steve Sanfield. Copyright © 1991 by Steve Sanfield. Used with permission of the publisher, Orchard Books, New York.

The Flame of Peace, by Deborah Nourse Lattimore. Copyright © 1987 by Deborah Nourse Lattimore. Selection reprinted by permission of HarperCollins Publishers.

"Harriet," from *Tales for the Perfect Child*, by Florence Parry Heide (pages 55–61). Text copyright © 1985 by Florence Parry Heide. By permission of Lothrop, Lee & Shepard Books, a division of William Morrow & Co., Inc.

How Tom Beat Captain Najork and His Hired Sportsmen, by Russell Hoban. Text copyright © 1974 by Russell Hoban. By permission of Wylie, Aitken, & Stone, Inc., 250 West 57th Street, New York, NY 10107.

It's New! It's Improved! It's Terrible!, by Stephen Manes. Copyright © 1989 by Stephen Manes. For performance rights, contact the Joanna Lewis Cole Literary Agency, 404 Riverside Drive, New York, NY 10025. Used by permission of Bantam Books, a division of Bantam Doubleday Dell Publishing Group, Inc.

The Jade Stone, by Caryn Yacowitz, published by Holiday House. Text copyright © 1992 by Caryn Yacowitz. Reprinted by permission of Curtis Brown, Ltd., Ten Astor Place, New York, NY 10003.

"Jumping Mouse," from *Seven Arrows* by Hyemeyohsts Storm. Copyright © 1972 by Hyemeyohsts Storm. Reprinted by permission of HarperCollins Publishers, Inc.

The Last Unicorn, by Peter S. Beagle. Copyright © 1968 by Peter S. Beagle. Reprinted by permission of McIntosh and Otis, Inc., 310 Madison Avenue, New York, NY 10017.

For Jean Wagner
and the Chamber Readers

Contents

WORLDS OF FANTASY
The following three scripts can be performed either separately or as a unified program of about 50 minutes.

About This Book

Reader's theater is widely viewed as a key tool in the move toward a literature-based curriculum. It encourages and develops reading skills in the context of a cooperative and fun activity, while requiring minimal equipment and set-up. It has been found invaluable in both language arts and social studies instruction.

Stories on Stage is a collection of reader's theater scripts based on quality literature and aimed primarily at students in the middle grades and junior high. The scripts may be freely copied for noncommercial, educational purposes. The book grew out of my professional experience in reader's theater between 1986 and 1991, including performing in schools, scripting, directing, and teaching workshops for both students and teachers.

I encourage the creation of scripts in the classroom and have included helpful hints on this in the appendix. However, teachers often tell me they would prefer to start with scripts ready-made. As a convenient source of high-quality reader's theater adaptations, *Stories on Stage* will help meet this need.

The primary goal of this collection is to promote reading. For enhancement of that function, I recommend having on hand one or more copies of the book that a script is based on, along with other books by the same author. But above all, have fun with the scripts. Let your readers discover that reading is a treat.

ABOUT THE SCRIPTS

The table of contents provides information to guide your script selection. For each title, you'll find notation on genre, culture of origin or setting, theme, grade level, number of roles, and approximate reading time. The grade level is only suggested, and applies to *performers*—the scripts can often be performed for audiences several years younger.

On the first page of each script is a list of roles. Multiple roles that might be assigned to a single reader are designated by a slash, as in "Role 1/Role 2." Of course, each such role can be assigned instead to an individual reader, and roles not so designated can often be combined.

Roles listed in parentheses are "silent," with no assigned speech, and usually optional. If your directing style includes stage movement, these roles can be given to surplus performers.

Though special effort has been made to include scripts with strong females, *Stories on Stage* still reflects the dominance of male characters in literature for both children and adults. I recommend that you compensate for this by casting females in male roles.

The script pages are designed to be photocopied for direct use by student readers. For performing, some kind of binder will be helpful.

ABOUT STAGING

Of course, an actual stage is not required for reader's theater. "Stage" here refers simply to the performing area, which might be the front of a classroom. (The scripts could also be used as group reading exercises, with no performing area at all.)

I suggest that you first read the scripts—or their source stories—*to* the young people. Many of these scripts will be a challenge, and effective modeling will lead to greater benefit and enjoyment.

The readers can underline or highlight their own parts in their copies of the scripts, marking only words to be spoken. (I recommend yellow nonfluorescent marker.) Any unfamiliar words should be looked up and checked for pronunciation and meaning. Your additional stage directions can go in the script margins—preferably in pencil, to allow for corrections.

The readers might also prepare introductions to the stories, for use in performance. Though an introduction should always mention the title and the author, it could also discuss source, author background, cultural background, theme, or context within a longer work. But it shouldn't give away the plot! Notes found at the beginning of some scripts will provide starting points. Introductions are most effective when spoken informally, rather than read or memorized exactly.

With most of these scripts, you can produce a lively stereo effect by dividing your narrators between the two ends of your stage. For instance, with four narrators, place Narrators 1 and 2 at far left (as you face the stage), and 3 and 4 at far right. To preserve this effect with fewer readers, assign the roles of Narrators 1 and 2 to one reader, and 3 and 4 to another.

In several scripts, particular narrators relate mostly to particular characters. Notes at the start of those scripts will suggest positioning the characters near the corresponding narrators.

There are many styles of reader's theater. In the most traditional style:

- Readers are arranged in a row or semicircle, sitting on high stools or standing.
- Scripts are often set on music stands.
- Readers look straight out toward the audience or at an angle, rather than looking at each other.
- Characters "exit" by turning their backs to the audience.

- Scene changes—jumps in time or place—can be shown by a group "freeze," followed by some kind of collective shift.

The group I performed with, though, had developed a style quite different, designed to appeal to young audiences:

- Characters move around the stage much as in a play, acting out or suggesting the movements described in the story, often by simple mime devices like walking in place.
- Though narrators look at the audience, characters most often look at each other.
- Scripts in sturdy binders are held in one hand, leaving the other hand free for gesturing.
- A set of low stools and a single high stool serve as versatile stage scenery/props.
- Exiting and scene changes are done more or less in the traditional way.

The scripts in this book should lend themselves to either approach, or to any other you might choose. Feel free to create your own! There *are* rules in reader's theater, but luckily there is no one to enforce them.

Thanks to Dan O'Gara for first giving me the idea for *Stories on Stage*. Thanks also to my editor, Judy O'Malley, whose enthusiasm and dedication to this project has at times exceeded my own.

I hope you find the scripts both rewarding and fun. Let me know how they work for you, by writing to me in care of the publisher. You're likely to get back a new script!

AARON SHEPARD

The Legend of Lightning Larry

By Aaron Shepard

From *The Legend of Lightning Larry*, Scribners, 1993

22+ ROLES: Citizen 1, Citizen 2, Citizen 3, Citizen 4, Citizen 5, Citizen 6, Citizen 7, Citizen 8, Lightning Larry, Crooked Curt, Evil-Eye McNeevil, Dismal Dan, Devilish Dick, Dreadful Dave, Stinky Steve, Sickening Sid, Raunchy Ralph, Grimy Greg, Creepy Cal, Moldy Mike, Lousy Luke, Gruesome Gus, (Other Citizens/Musicians/Bartender/Bank Teller)

8 minutes

NOTE: CITIZENS serve as narrators. If possible, all readers should speak with a Western drawl.

CITIZEN 1: Well, you've heard about gunfighting good guys like Wild Bill Hickok and Wyatt Earp.

CITIZEN 8: But we'll tell you a name that strikes even greater fear into the hearts of bad men everywhere.

ALL (except LARRY): Lightning Larry!

CITIZEN 2: We'll never forget the day Larry rode into our little town of Brimstone and walked into the Cottonmouth Saloon. He strode up to the bar, smiled straight at the bartender, and said,

LIGHTNING LARRY: Lemonade, please!

CITIZEN 7: Every head in the place turned to look.

CITIZEN 3: Now, standing next to Larry at the bar was Crooked Curt.

CITIZEN 6: Curt was one of a band of rustlers and thieves that had been terrorizing our town, led by a ferocious outlaw named Evil-Eye McNeevil.

CITIZEN 4: Curt was wearing the usual outlaw scowl.

CITIZEN 5: Larry turned to him and smiled.

LIGHTNING LARRY: Mighty big frown you got there, mister!

CROOKED CURT: What's it to *you?*

LIGHTNING LARRY: Well, maybe I could help remove it!

CROOKED CURT: I'd like to see you try!

CITIZEN 1: The rest of us got out of the way, real fast.

CITIZEN 8: The bartender ducked behind the bar.

CITIZEN 2: Larry and Curt moved about ten paces from each other, hands at the ready.

CITIZEN 7: Larry was still smiling.

CITIZEN 3: Curt moved first. But he only just cleared his gun from its holster before Larry aimed and fired.

LIGHTNING LARRY: *Zing!*

CITIZEN 6: There was no bang and no bullet. Just a little bolt of light that hit Curt right in the heart.

CITIZEN 4: Curt just stood there, his eyes wide with surprise. Then he dropped his gun, and a huge grin spread over his face.

CITIZEN 5: He rushed up to Larry and pumped his hand.

CROOKED CURT: I'm mighty glad to know you, stranger! The drinks are on me! Lemonade for everyone!

* * *

CITIZEN 1: When Evil-Eye McNeevil and his outlaw gang heard that Crooked Curt had gone straight, they shuddered right down to their boots.

CITIZEN 8: Most any outlaw would rather die than smile!

CITIZEN 2: Evil-Eye's men were shook up, but they weren't about to let on.

CITIZEN 7: The very next day,

DISMAL DAN: Dismal Dan!

DEVILISH DICK: Devilish Dick!

DREADFUL DAVE: and Dreadful Dave!

CITIZEN 7: rode into Brimstone, yelling like crazy men and shooting wild.

DAN, DICK, & DAVE: *(hoot and holler, prance, wave guns and shoot)*

CITIZEN 3: Windows shattered

CITIZEN 6: and citizens scattered.

CITIZEN 4: Then Lightning Larry showed up. He never warned them.

CITIZEN 5: Never even stopped smiling.

CITIZEN 1: Just shot three little bolts of light.

LIGHTNING LARRY: *Zing! Zing! Zing!*

DAN, DICK, & DAVE: *(stop and fall when hit)*

CITIZEN 8: Hit those outlaws right in the heart.

CITIZEN 2: Larry's shots knocked the outlaws to the ground. They lay there trying to figure out what had hit them. Then they got up and looked around.

DISMAL DAN: Looks like we did some damage, boys.

CITIZEN 7: . . . said Dismal Dan.

DEVILISH DICK: Hope nobody got hurt!

CITIZEN 3: . . . said Devilish Dick.

DREADFUL DAVE: We'd better get to work and fix this place up.

CITIZEN 6: . . . said Dreadful Dave.

CITIZEN 4: They spent the rest of the day replacing windows and apologizing to everyone who'd listen.

CITIZEN 5: Then for good measure, they picked up all the trash in the street.

* * *

CITIZEN 1: Evil-Eye McNeevil had lost three more of his meanest men,

CITIZEN 8: and he was furious!

CITIZEN 2: He decided to do something *really* nasty.

CITIZEN 7: The next day,

STINKY STEVE: Stinky Steve!

SICKENING SID: and Sickening Sid!

CITIZEN 7: walked into the 79th National Savings and Loan, with guns in hand.

CITIZEN 3: They wore masks,

CITIZEN 6: but everyone knew who they were—from the smell.

STINKY STEVE: Stick up your hands.

CITIZEN 4: . . . said Stinky Steve.

SICKENING SID: Give us all the money in your vault.

CITIZEN 5: . . . ordered Sickening Sid.

CITIZEN 1: They were just backing out the door with the money bags, when Lightning Larry strolled by.

CITIZEN 8: Didn't even slow his step.

CITIZEN 2: Just shot those bandits in the back.

LIGHTNING LARRY: *Zing! Zing!*

CITIZEN 7: Went right through to the heart.

CITIZEN 3: The puzzled outlaws stopped and looked at each other.

STINKY STEVE: Seems a shame to steal the money of hardworking cowboys.

SICKENING SID: Wouldn't want to make their lives any harder.

CITIZEN 6: They holstered their guns and walked back to the teller.

CITIZEN 4: They plunked the money bags down on the counter.

SICKENING SID: Now, you keep that money safe.

CITIZEN 5: Then they pulled out their wallets and opened up accounts.

* * *

CITIZEN 1: That was the last straw for Evil-Eye McNeevil. It was time for a showdown!

CITIZEN 8: The next day, at high noon, Larry was sipping lemonade at the Cottonmouth Saloon. Evil-Eye burst through the doors and stamped up to him.

EVIL-EYE McNEEVIL: I'm Evil-Eye McNeevil!

LIGHTNING LARRY: *(with a huge smile)* Hello, Evil-Eye! Can I buy you a lemonade?

EVIL-EYE McNEEVIL: This town ain't big enough for the both of us.

LIGHTNING LARRY: Seems pretty spacious to me!

EVIL-EYE McNEEVIL: I'll be waiting for you, down by the Okey-Dokey Corral.

CITIZEN 8: And Evil-Eye stamped out.

CITIZEN 2: Larry finished his lemonade and walked out onto Main Street.

CITIZEN 7: Evil-Eye was waiting for him. But Evil-Eye wasn't alone.

CITIZEN 3: There on either side of him were

RAUNCHY RALPH: Raunchy Ralph!

GRIMY GREG: Grimy Greg!

CREEPY CAL: Creepy Cal!

MOLDY MIKE: Moldy Mike!

LOUSY LUKE: Lousy Luke!

GRUESOME GUS: And Gruesome Gus!

CITIZEN 6: And not a one of them looked friendly.

LIGHTNING LARRY: Nice day for a stroll!

CITIZEN 4: . . . called Larry.

EVIL-EYE McNEEVIL: Draw!

CITIZEN 5: . . . said Evil-Eye.

CITIZEN 1: All of us citizens of Brimstone were lining Main Street to see what would happen.

CITIZEN 8: Larry was still smiling, but we knew even Larry couldn't outshoot all those outlaws together.

CITIZEN 2: Just then, a voice came from the Cottonmouth Saloon.

CROOKED CURT: Like some help, Larry?

LIGHTNING LARRY: Wouldn't mind it!

CITIZEN 7: Out stepped . . . Crooked Curt! And right behind him were Dismal Dan, Devilish Dick, Dreadful Dave, Stinky Steve, and Sickening Sid.

CITIZEN 3: They all took places beside Larry.

CROOKED CURT: Hello, Evil-Eye!

CITIZEN 6: . . . called Curt.

EVIL-EYE McNEEVIL: Traitors!

CITIZEN 4: . . . yelled Evil-Eye.

LIGHTNING LARRY: Draw!

CITIZEN 5: . . . said Larry, with a smile.

CITIZEN 1: Evil-Eye and his men drew their guns,

CITIZEN 8: but Larry and his friends were an eye-blink quicker.

CITIZEN 2: Their guns fired seven little bolts of light.

LARRY & FRIENDS: *Zing!*

CITIZEN 7: Hit those outlaws right in the you-know-what.

EVIL-EYE McNEEVIL: YIPPEE!

CITIZEN 3: . . . yelled Evil-Eye.

CITIZEN 6: He shot in the air.

EVIL-EYE McNEEVIL: *Zing!*

CITIZEN 4: There was no bang and no bullet.

CITIZEN 5: Just a little bolt of light.

LIGHTNING LARRY: All right, men! Let's clean up this town, once and for all!

LARRY & ALL OUTLAWS: *(shoot at all others)* *Zing! Zing! Zing!* . . .

CITIZEN 1: And before we could duck for cover,

CITIZEN 8: Larry and Evil-Eye and the others

CITIZEN 2: turned their guns on the *rest* of us.

CITIZEN 7: Bolts of light flew everywhere.

CITIZEN 3: *No* one was spared—

CITIZEN 6: not a man,

CITIZEN 4: woman,

CITIZEN 5: or child!

ALL (except LARRY): YIPPEE!

CITIZEN 1: You never saw such a happy crowd!

CITIZEN 8: We all rushed around

CITIZEN 2: and pumped each other's hands

CITIZEN 7: and hugged each other.

CITIZEN 3: Then the musicians got out instruments, and we had dancing, too.

CITIZEN 6: Main Street was one huge party,

CITIZEN 4: all the rest of that day,

CITIZEN 5: and on through the night.

CITIZEN 1: We never drank so much lemonade in all our days!

* * *

CITIZEN 1: With all the commotion, only a few of us saw Larry ride into the sunset.

CITIZEN 8: Can't say where he went.

CITIZEN 2: Can't say what he's doing now.

CITIZEN 7: But we bet he still aims for the heart.

ALL: (*shooting at audience*) Zing!

Harriet

By Florence Parry Heide

From *Tales for the Perfect Child*, Lothrop, Lee and Shepard, 1985

6 ROLES: Narrator 1, Narrator 2, Narrator 3, Narrator 4, Harriet, Mother

3 minutes

NARRATOR 1: Harriet was a very good whiner. She practiced and practiced, and so of course she got better and better at it.

NARRATOR 4: Practice makes perfect.

NARRATOR 2: Some children hardly *ever* whine. Can you believe that?

NARRATOR 3: So of course, they never get to be very *good* at it.

HARRIET: Can I have a piece of that blueberry pie?

NARRATOR 1: . . . Harriet asked her mother while her mother was fixing dinner.

NARRATOR 4: Guests were coming, and her mother wanted everything to be very nice.

MOTHER: No, Harriet. The pie is for after dinner. We're having roast beef.

NARRATOR 2: Children like Harriet are not interested in roast beef when they are interested in pie.

NARRATOR 3: Harriet used her best whiny voice.

HARRIET: I want a piece of *pie.*

MOTHER: I said no, and I mean no.

NARRATOR 1: Harriet's mother always liked to say what she meant.

NARRATOR 4: She started to make some nice tomato aspic.

HARRIET: Can I have some *pie,* can I have some *pie?*

MOTHER: Harriet, I told you, when I say no, I mean no!

HARRIET: But I want some *pie.*

MOTHER: Harriet—

HARRIET: Can I have some *pie?*

NARRATOR 2: Harriet's mother tried to concentrate on the aspic—

HARRIET: *Please* can I have some *pie?*

NARRATOR 2: but that was very hard to do, because Harriet was whining.

HARRIET: Why won't you give me some *pie? Why? Why? (whimpers)*

NARRATOR 3: Good whiners make it very hard for anyone to think of anything else.

MOTHER: Why don't you color in your nice new coloring book?

HARRIET: I want some pie *now.*

MOTHER: Dinner will be ready pretty soon.

HARRIET: But *I* want some pie NOW.

NARRATOR 1: A good whiner sticks to one subject.

HARRIET: *I want some pie.*

NARRATOR 4: A good whiner never gives up.

HARRIET: PLEASE can I have some *pie?*

NARRATOR 2: Harriet kept whining—

HARRIET: I want some *pie.* I want some *pie.* I want some *pie.*

NARRATOR 2: and her mother kept trying to get dinner ready.

HARRIET: *I . . . want . . . some . . .* PIE.

NARRATOR 3: Her mother burned the gravy.

MOTHER: (*shouting*) All right, all right! Have some PIE!

NARRATOR 1: She was very tired of hearing Harriet whine.

NARRATOR 4: Harriet stopped whining while she had her piece of pie.

NARRATOR 2: She always rested up between whines.

NARRATOR 3: That's what good whiners always do.

Millions of Cats

By Wanda Gag

Adapted from *Millions of Cats*, Putnam & Grosset, 1988 (first published by Coward-McCann, 1928)

9+ ROLES: Narrator 1, Narrator 2, Narrator 3, Narrator 4, Old Man, Old Woman, Kitty, Cats

6 minutes

NARRATOR 1: Once upon a time, there was

OLD MAN: a very old man.

OLD WOMAN: And a very old woman.

NARRATOR 4: They lived in a nice clean house that had flowers all around it,

NARRATOR 2: except where the door was. But they couldn't be happy,

NARRATOR 3: because they were so very lonely.

OLD WOMAN: If we only had a cat!

NARRATOR 1: . . . sighed the very old woman.

OLD MAN: A cat?

NARRATOR 4: . . . asked the very old man.

OLD WOMAN: Yes, a sweet little fluffy cat.

NARRATOR 2: . . . said the very old woman.

OLD MAN: I will get you a cat, my dear.

NARRATOR 3: . . . said the very old man. And he set out to look for one.

NARRATOR 1: He climbed over the sunny hills.

NARRATOR 4: He trudged through the cool valleys.

NARRATOR 2: He walked a long, long time,

NARRATOR 3: and at last he came to a hill which was quite covered with cats.

CATS & KITTY: Mew, mew, mew. . . .

NARRATOR 1: Cats *here*,

NARRATOR 4: cats *there*,

NARRATORS 2 & 3: cats and kittens *everywhere*.

NARRATOR 1: *Hundreds* of cats,

NARRATOR 4: *thousands* of cats,

NARRATOR 2: *millions*

NARRATOR 2 & 3: and BILLIONS

NARRATORS 1, 2, 3, 4: and *TRILLIONS* of cats.

OLD MAN: Oh! Now I can choose the prettiest cat and take it home with me!

NARRATOR 1: So he chose one. It was white. But just as he was about to leave,

NARRATOR 4: he saw another one, all black and white, and it seemed just as pretty as the first. So he took this one also. But then he saw

NARRATOR 2: a fuzzy gray kitten way over here, which was every bit as pretty as the others. So he took it too. And now he saw,

NARRATOR 3: way down in a corner, one which he thought too lovely to leave. So he took this too. And just then,

NARRATOR 1: over here, the very old man found a kitten which was black and very beautiful.

OLD MAN: It would be a shame to leave *that* one.

NARRATOR 1: So he took it. And now, over there,

NARRATOR 4: he saw a cat which had brown and yellow stripes like a baby tiger.

OLD MAN: I simply must take it!

NARRATOR 4: And he did.

NARRATOR 2: And so it happened

NARRATOR 3: that every time the very old man looked up,

NARRATOR 1: he saw another cat which was so pretty,

NARRATOR 4: he could not bear to leave it.

NARRATOR 2: Before he knew it,

NARRATOR 3: he had chosen them all!

CATS & KITTY: Mew, mew, mew. . . .

NARRATOR 1: And so he went back over the sunny hills,

NARRATOR 4: and down through the cool valleys,

NARRATOR 2: to show all the pretty kittens

NARRATOR 3: to the very old woman.

NARRATOR 1: And all the hundreds of cats,

NARRATOR 4: thousands of cats,

NARRATOR 2: millions

NARRATOR 2 & 3: and billions

NARRATORS 1, 2, 3, 4: and trillions of cats

NARRATOR 1: followed him.

CATS & KITTY: Mew, mew, mew. . . .

NARRATOR 1: They came to a pond.

CATS & KITTY: Mew, mew! We are thirsty!

NARRATOR 1: . . . cried the hundreds of cats,

NARRATOR 4: thousands of cats,

NARRATOR 2: millions

NARRATOR 2 & 3: and billions

NARRATORS 1, 2, 3, 4: and trillions of cats.

OLD MAN: Well, here is a great deal of water.

NARRATOR 4: . . . said the very old man.

NARRATOR 2: Each cat took a sip of water.

CATS & KITTY: (sip)

NARRATOR 3: The pond was gone!

CATS & KITTY: Mew, mew! Now we are hungry!

NARRATOR 1: . . . cried the hundreds of cats,

NARRATOR 4: thousands of cats,

NARRATOR 2: millions

NARRATOR 2 & 3: and billions

NARRATORS 1, 2, 3, 4: and trillions of cats.

OLD MAN: There is much grass on the hills.

NARRATOR 4: . . . said the very old man.

NARRATOR 2: Each cat ate a mouthful of grass.

CATS & KITTY: (chew)

NARRATOR 3: Not a blade was left!

CATS & KITTY: Mew, mew, mew. . . .

NARRATOR 1: Pretty soon, the very old woman saw them coming.

OLD WOMAN: My dear! What are you doing? I asked for one little cat, and what do I see?
Cats here,
Cats there,
Cats and kittens everywhere!
Hundreds of cats,
Thousands of cats,
Millions and billions and trillions of cats!
But we can never *feed* them all. They will eat us out of house and home!

OLD MAN: I never thought of that!

NARRATOR 4: . . . said the very old man.

OLD MAN: What shall we do?

NARRATOR 2: The very old woman thought for a while.

OLD WOMAN: *I* know! We will let the *cats* decide which one we should keep.

OLD MAN: Oh, yes!

NARRATOR 3: And the very old man called to the cats,

OLD MAN: Which one of you is the prettiest?

CATS: *I* am! . . . No, *I* am! . . . No, *I* am the prettiest! . . .

NARRATOR 1: . . . cried the hundreds of cats,

NARRATOR 4: thousands of cats,

NARRATOR 2: millions

NARRATOR 2 & 3: and billions

NARRATORS 1, 2, 3, 4: and trillions of cats,

NARRATOR 1: for each cat thought *it* was the prettiest.

CATS: *I* am! . . . No, *I* am! . . . No, *I* am the prettiest! . . .

NARRATOR 1: And they began to quarrel. They bit

NARRATOR 4: and scratched

NARRATOR 2: and clawed each other

NARRATOR 3: and made such a great noise

NARRATOR 1: that the very old man

NARRATOR 4: and the very old woman

NARRATOR 2: ran into the house

NARRATOR 3: as fast as they could.

CATS: *I* am! . . . No, *I* am! . . . No, *I* am the prettiest! . . .

NARRATOR 1: But after awhile the noise stopped. The very old man

NARRATOR 4: and the very old woman

NARRATOR 2: peeped out to see what had happened.

NARRATOR 3: They could not see a single cat!

OLD WOMAN: I think they must have eaten each other all up. It's too bad!

OLD MAN: But look!

NARRATOR 1: The very old man pointed to a bunch of high grass.

NARRATOR 4: In it sat one little frightened kitten.

NARRATOR 2: They went out and picked it up.

NARRATOR 3: It was thin and scraggly.

OLD WOMAN: Poor little kitty.

OLD MAN: *Dear* little kitty, how does it happen that you were not eaten up with all those hundreds and thousands and millions and billions and trillions of cats?

KITTY: Oh, I'm just a very homely little cat. So when you asked who was the prettiest, I didn't say anything. So nobody bothered about me.

NARRATOR 1: They took the kitten into the house.

NARRATOR 4: The very old woman gave it a warm bath and brushed its fur until it was soft and shiny.

NARRATOR 2: Every day, they gave it plenty of milk,

NARRATOR 3: and soon it grew nice and plump.

OLD WOMAN: And it is a very pretty cat, after all!

OLD MAN: It is the most beautiful cat in the whole world! I ought to know, for I've seen

Hundreds of cats,
Thousands of cats,
Millions and billions and trillions of cats!

And not *one* was as pretty as *this*.

Mr. Bim's Bamboo

By Carol Farley

Adapted from "Mr. Bim's Bamboo," in *Cricket: The Magazine for Children*,
January 1989

**8 ROLES: Narrator 1, Narrator 2, Mr. Bim, Friend, Man, Boy,
Woman 1, Woman 2**

6 minutes

NOTE: This is an original story based on elements of East Asian culture.

NARRATOR 1: Mr. Bim had a bamboo garden and a bamboo shop in a
small village by a large mountain. He was old, and his face had more
wrinkles than the mountain had trees. But he wore a shining white suit,
and he always looked fine.

NARRATOR 2: His bamboo was fine too, and his shop was filled with useful
things.

BIM:
I have bamboo trays and bamboo hats,
Bamboo pots and bamboo mats.
Bamboo frames and bamboo poles,
Bamboo rugs and bamboo bowls.

Try Bim's bamboo!

NARRATOR 1: People would hurry inside and buy.

FRIEND: Mr. Bim has the best bamboo in all the world!

NARRATOR 2: . . . they told each other, smiling and nodding and bowing.
This made Mr. Bim feel so good, his head nearly touched the ground as he
bowed.

NARRATOR 1: Then one morning, some people came from the other side of the mountain.

BIM:

I have the best, as you can see.
Come and buy bamboo from me!

WOMAN 1: (sneering) Bim's bamboo. Foo!

NARRATOR 2: Mr. Bim's smile disappeared as quickly as a butterfly in a windstorm.

MAN: Bamboo is old! We want new things, modern things.

WOMAN 1: In our city, we buy plastic. Bim's bamboo. Foo!

BIM: I've never heard of "plass-tick." Where does it grow?

MAN: Plastic doesn't grow! Plastic must be made.

WOMAN 1: Nobody wants bamboo. It's old and useless!

MAN: New things are always better!

NARRATOR 1: Soon all the people in the village were talking about the plastic from the other side of the mountain. They wanted plastic things, too. So they went to new shops.

NARRATOR 2: Mr. Bim's friend told him,

FRIEND: You must change your ways. You must become modern. Go over the mountain to the factories, and buy new things to sell in your shop.

BIM: I am old like a turtle, and my ways are like a turtle shell—they make me what I am. Anyway, I don't think old things are always useless!

NARRATOR 1: As the months and years passed, Mr. Bim stayed near his quiet shop on the empty street.

NARRATOR 2: He took care of his lovely garden, kept his white coat and trousers shining, and dusted his beautiful bamboo. But no one came to buy.

NARRATOR 1: One day, after all the people had moved away from the small village, Mr. Bim stopped dusting his bamboo.

BIM: It's foolish. No one will ever buy it again. Just like me, it's old and useless.

NARRATOR 2: Mr. Bim closed the door of his shop and sat down. He looked at the mountains far off in the distance.

NARRATOR 1: He saw that, in the wintertime, the mountaintops were covered with glistening white snow.

NARRATOR 2: Every spring, the snow melted into sparkling waterfalls.

NARRATOR 1: During the hot summer months, the water disappeared.

NARRATOR 2: But then, in late fall and winter, the snow came back to the mountaintops, glistening white and beautiful, the same as before.

NARRATOR 1: The old became new,

NARRATOR 2: and the new became old.

BIM: I believe the mountains are trying to *tell* me something.

NARRATOR 1: Mr. Bim opened his shop door. Humming and smiling, he began dusting his beautiful bamboo.

NARRATOR 2: Just then, a little boy ran into the shop.

BOY: What's this?

NARRATOR 1: He picked up a bamboo whistle and blew it.

BOY: *(whistles)* Mommy! Come listen to this beautiful whistle!

NARRATOR 2: A young woman with travel bags hurried inside.

WOMAN 2: We must hurry on with the others. You have *many* whistles. You don't need another.

BOY: But this is different!

WOMAN 2: Different? *(looks around the shop)* My goodness! None of these things are plastic! *(to Bim)* What are they made of?

BIM: *(smiling)* Bamboo!

WOMAN 2: "Bam-boo"? I've never *heard* of it. Is it new?

BIM: No, it's old!

WOMAN 2: What factory makes it?

BIM: Bamboo grows! I have bamboo plants in my garden, and I made these bamboo things myself!

WOMAN 2: It *grows*? And you make all these beautiful things *yourself*? This is a miracle! A *miracle!*

BIM: *(bowing)* The old is not always useless. The new is not always best.

WOMAN 2: I must tell the others about these treasures! *(to others outside)* Over here! Quickly! You must see this!

NARRATOR 1: Soon Mr. Bim's shop was full of people.

MAN: Beautiful!

WOMAN 1: A miracle!

MAN: And what do you suppose? Bamboo *grows!*

NARRATOR 2: As people began buying his bamboo, Mr. Bim smiled and nodded.

BIM:

I have bamboo trays and bamboo hats,
Bamboo pots and bamboo mats.
Bamboo frames and bamboo poles,
Bamboo rugs and bamboo bowls.

Some useful things are old.
Some useful things are new.
But what can be both old and new?

ALL:

Bim's bam-boo!

Talk

A tall tale of West Africa, retold by Harold Courlander and George Herzog

Adapted from "Talk," in *The Cow-Tail Switch, and Other West African Stories,* Henry Holt, 1947

15–16 ROLES: Narrator 1, Narrator 2, Yam, (Cow), Dog, Tree, Branch, Stone, Fisherman, Trap, Weaver, Cloth, Bather, River, Chief, Stool

4 minutes

NOTE: Harold Courlander heard this story in Nigeria, told by an Ashanti from Ghana. For additional background, see the notes at the end of *The Cowtail Switch.* For best effect, each talking animal or object should have a distinctive funny voice, and the human characters should imitate them while describing what they said.

NARRATOR 1: Once, not far from the city of Accra, a man went out to his garden to dig up some yams to take to market. While he was digging, one of the yams said to him,

YAM: So, you're finally here! You never weeded me, but now you come around with your digging stick. Go away and *leave me alone!*

NARRATOR 2: The farmer turned around and looked at his cow in amazement. The cow was chewing her cud and looking at *him.*

FARMER: Did you *say* something?

NARRATOR 2: The cow kept chewing and said nothing. But the man's *dog* spoke up.

DOG: It wasn't the cow who spoke to you. It was the yam! The yam says leave him alone!

NARRATOR 1: The man became angry, because his dog had never talked before, and he didn't like its tone, besides. So he took his knife and cut a branch from a palm tree to whip his dog. But then the *palm* tree said,

TREE: Put that branch down!

NARRATOR 2: The man was getting upset. He was just about to throw the branch away, when the *branch* said,

BRANCH: Man, put me down softly!

NARRATOR 1: He put the branch down gently on a stone. But the *stone* said,

STONE: Hey! Take that thing off me!

FARMER: *(freaking out)* WAH!

NARRATOR 2: The frightened farmer started to run for his village. On the way, he met a fisherman carrying along a fish trap on his head.

FISHERMAN: What's the hurry?

FARMER: The yam said, "Leave me alone!" The dog said, "Listen to the yam!" The tree said, "Put that branch down!" The branch said, "Do it softly!" And the stone said, "Take that thing off me!"

FISHERMAN: Is that all? Is that so frightening?

TRAP: Well?

NARRATOR 2: . . . said the man's fish trap.

TRAP: Did he take the branch off the stone?

FARMER & FISHERMAN: WAH!

NARRATOR 1: The fisherman threw down the fish trap and began to run with the farmer. On the trail, they met a weaver with a bundle of cloth on his head.

WEAVER: Why are you in such a rush?

FARMER: The yam said, "Leave me alone!" The dog said, "Listen to the yam!" The tree said, "Put that branch down!" The branch said, "Do it softly!" The stone said, "Take that thing off me!"

FISHERMAN: And the trap said, "Did he take it off?"

WEAVER: *That's* nothing to get excited about. No reason at all!

CLOTH: Oh, yes, it is!

NARRATOR 1: . . . said the bundle of cloth.

CLOTH: If it happened to *you*, you'd run too!

FARMER, FISHERMAN, & WEAVER: WAH!

NARRATOR 2: The weaver threw down his bundle and ran with the other men. They came panting to the ford in the river, and found a man taking a bath.

BATHER: Why are you running like that? Are you chasing a gazelle?

FARMER: The yam said, "Leave me alone!" The dog said, "Listen to the yam!" The tree said, "Put that branch down!" The branch said, "Do it softly!" The stone said, "Take that thing off me!"

FISHERMAN: The trap said, "Did he take it off?"

WEAVER: And the cloth said, "You'd run too!"

BATHER: And that made you run?

RIVER: Well, why not?

NARRATOR 2: . . . said the river.

RIVER: Wouldn't *you* run, if it were you?

FARMER, FISHERMAN, WEAVER, & BATHER: WAH!

NARRATOR 1: The man jumped naked out of the water, and began to run with the others. They ran into the village and down the main street, till they reached the house of the chief.

NARRATOR 2: The chief brought out his royal stool, and sat on it to listen to their complaints. The men began to recite their troubles.

FARMER: I went out to my garden to dig yams. Then everything began to talk! The yam said, "Leave me alone!" The dog said, "Listen to the yam!" The tree said, "Put that branch down!" The branch said, "Do it softly!" The stone said, "Take that thing off me!"

FISHERMAN: The trap said, "Did he take it off?"

WEAVER: The cloth said, "You'd run too!"

BATHER: And the river said, "Wouldn't you?"

NARRATOR 1: The chief listened patiently at first, but finally grew annoyed.

CHIEF: Now, this is a really wild story. Go back to your work, *all* of you, before I punish you for disturbing the peace!

FARMER, FISHERMAN, WEAVER, BATHER: *(back off fearfully and leave)*

NARRATOR 2: So the men went away. The chief shook his head.

CHIEF: That kind of nonsense upsets the community.

STOOL: Ridiculous, isn't it!

NARRATOR 2: . . . said his royal stool.

STOOL: Imagine! A talking yam!

CHIEF: WAH!

The Jade Stone

A Chinese folktale, adapted by Caryn Yacowitz

From *The Jade Stone: A Chinese Folktale*, Holiday House, 1992

11+ ROLES: Narrator 1, Narrator 2, Narrator 3, Narrator 4, Chan Lo, Emperor, Stone, Adviser 1, Adviser 2, Adviser 3, Apprentice, (Emperor's Men/Guards)

10 minutes

NARRATOR 1: Long ago in China there lived a stone carver named

CHAN LO: *(bowing)* Chan Lo.

NARRATOR 4: Chan Lo spent his days carving birds and deer and water buffalo from the colored stones he found near the river.

NARRATOR 2: His young apprentice asked,

APPRENTICE: How do you know what to carve?

CHAN LO: I always listen to the stone.

NARRATOR 3: . . . replied Chan Lo.

CHAN LO: The stone tells me what it wants to be.

NARRATOR 1: People came from near and far to buy Chan Lo's carvings.

NARRATOR 4: So it happened that when the Great Emperor of All China was given a perfect piece of green-and-white jade stone, one of the advisers in the Celestial Palace thought of

ADVISER 1: Chan Lo!

NARRATOR 2: The humble stone carver was brought before the Great Emperor of All China. Chan Lo bowed deeply.

EMPEROR: I want you to carve a dragon.

NARRATOR 3: . . . the emperor commanded.

EMPEROR: A dragon of wind and fire.

CHAN LO: I will do my best to please you.

NARRATOR 1: The emperor's men carried the precious stone to Chan Lo's garden.

NARRATOR 4: Chan Lo had never seen such a perfect piece of jade. The green-and-white of the stone was like moss-entangled-in-snow.

NARRATOR 2: The great emperor had commanded, "a dragon of wind and fire." Chan Lo wondered if that was what the stone wanted to be. He spoke to it.

CHAN LO:
Here I stand, O Noble Stone,
to carve a creature of your own.
Whisper signs and sounds from rock
that I, your servant, may unlock.

NARRATOR 3: Chan Lo bent down and put his ear to the stone. From deep inside came a gentle sound.

STONE: (*softly*) Pah-tah. Pah-tah. Pah-*tah*.

CHAN LO: Do dragons make that sound?

NARRATOR 1: . . . Chan Lo wondered.

CHAN LO: Perhaps the dragon's tail splashing in the ocean says "Pah-tah, pah-*tah*."

NARRATOR 4: But he was not sure.

NARRATOR 2: That evening, Chan Lo thought about dragons.

NARRATOR 3: But late at night, in his dreams, he heard,

STONE: Pah-tah. Pah-tah.

STONE & CHAN LO: Pah-*tah*.

NARRATOR 1: The next morning, Chan Lo went to the garden.

NARRATOR 4: The stone was spring-water-green in the morning light.

CHAN LO:
Here I stand, O Noble Stone,
to carve a creature of your own.
Whisper signs and sounds from rock
that I, your servant, may unlock.

NARRATOR 2: Chan Lo put his ear to the green-and-white jade and listened.

NARRATOR 3: Softly the sounds came.

STONE: *(softly)* Bub-bub-bubble. Bub-bub-bubble.

CHAN LO: Do dragons make that sound?

NARRATOR 1: . . . Chan Lo asked himself.

CHAN LO: Perhaps a dragon rising from the wild waves blows bubbles through his nostrils.

NARRATOR 4: But these were not mighty dragon bubbles that were coming from the rock. They were gentle, lazy, playful sounds.

NARRATOR 2: That evening, Chan Lo tried again to think about dragons.

NARRATOR 3: But when he went to bed, he heard in his dreams the sound of

STONE: Bub-bub-bubble. Bub-bub-bubble.

STONE & CHAN LO: Bub-bub-bubble.

NARRATOR 1: In the middle of the night, Chan Lo awoke. He walked into the moonlit garden.

NARRATOR 4: The stone shone silvery-green in the moonlight.

CHAN LO:
Here I stand, O Noble Stone,
to carve a creature of your own.
Whisper signs and sounds from rock
that I, your servant, may unlock.

NARRATOR 2: He put his ear to the stone. Silence.

NARRATOR 3: Chan Lo ran his hands over the jade. His fingers felt tiny ridges, and the ridges made a sound.

STONE: (*softly*) S-s-s-ah, S-s-s-s-ah, S-s-s-s-s-s-ah.

CHAN LO: Do dragons have ridges?

NARRATOR 1: . . . Chan Lo pondered.

CHAN LO: Yes. They have scales. Scales on their tails and bodies. And their scales *might* say, "S-s-s-ah, S-s-s-s-ah, S-s-s-s-s-s-ah," if one dared to touch them.

NARRATOR 4: But Chan Lo knew these small, delicate ridges were *not* dragon scales.

NARRATOR 2: Chan Lo could not carve what he did not hear, but he was afraid to disobey the emperor.

NARRATOR 3: His fear weighed in him like a great stone as he picked up his tools and began to carve.

* * *

NARRATOR 1: Chan Lo worked slowly and carefully for a year and a day.

NARRATOR 4: Finally, the carving was complete.

NARRATOR 2: Early in the morning, before the birds were awake, Chan Lo and his apprentice wrapped the jade carving in a cloth and set out for the Celestial Palace.

NARRATOR 3: Chan Lo entered the Great Hall, where the three advisers sat waiting for the Great Emperor of All China. He placed the jade stone on the table in the center of the room.

NARRATOR 1: Soon the emperor's advisers grew curious. They scurried to the jade stone and peeked under the cloth.

ADVISER 1: (*surprised*) No dragon!

ADVISER 2: (*louder*) No dragon!

ADVISER 3: *(loudest)* NO DRAGON!

NARRATOR 4: At that moment, the emperor himself entered the Great Hall.

EMPEROR: Show me my dragon of wind and fire!

NARRATOR 2: The advisers whisked the cloth away.

EMPEROR: *(thundering) This* is not my dragon!

ADVISER 1: *(pointing at Chan Lo)* Punish him!

ADVISER 2: *Punish him!*

ADVISER 3: PUNISH HIM!

NARRATOR 3: Chan Lo's knees shook like ginkgo leaves in the wind.

CHAN LO: O mighty emperor, there *is* no dragon of wind and fire. I did not *hear* it! I heard these three carp fish swimming playfully in the reeds in the pool of the Celestial Palace.

EMPEROR: *Hear* them? You did not *hear* them!

ADVISER 1: Chop off his head!

ADVISER 2: *Boil him in oil!*

ADVISER 3: CUT HIM IN A THOUSAND PIECES!

NARRATOR 1: But the emperor was so angry, he could not decide which punishment to choose.

EMPEROR: I will let my *dreams* decide his punishment. Now, take him away! And remove that stone from the Celestial Palace!

NARRATOR 4: Chan Lo was dragged down many flights of stairs and thrown into a black prison cell. The carving was placed outside, near the reeds of the reflecting pool.

* * *

NARRATOR 2: That evening, the emperor thought about dragons.

NARRATOR 3: But late that night, in his sleep, the emperor dreamed of fish playfully slapping their tails in green water.

STONE: Pah-tah. Pah-tah.

STONE & EMPEROR: Pah-*tah*.

NARRATOR 1: In the morning, the emperor's advisers asked,

ADVISER 1: What punishment have you chosen?

NARRATOR 4: But the emperor said,

EMPEROR: My dreams have not yet decided.

NARRATOR 2: That evening, the emperor again tried to think about dragons.

NARRATOR 3: But when he went to bed, the emperor dreamed of fish gliding smoothly through deep, clear water.

STONE: Bub-bub-bubble. Bub-bub-bubble.

STONE & EMPEROR: Bub-bub-bubble.

NARRATOR 1: In the morning, the emperor's advisers again asked him,

ADVISER 2: What punishment have your dreams chosen?

NARRATOR 4: But the emperor told them,

EMPEROR: My dreams have still not decided.

NARRATOR 2: On the third night, the emperor groaned and tossed in his sleep, but he did not dream.

NARRATOR 3: He awoke in the darkest hour of the night. A strange sound filled the room.

STONE: S-s-s-ah, S-s-s-s-ah, S-s-s-s-s-s-ah.

NARRATOR 1: The emperor got out of bed and went toward the sound. He hurried down the corridors, through the Great Hall, and out into the moonlit garden.

NARRATOR 4: There by the reflecting pool was the jade stone. Next to it stood the apprentice, running his fingers down the scales of the three carp fish.

STONE: S-s-s-ah, S-s-s-s-ah, S-s-s-s-s-s-ah.

NARRATOR 2: When the apprentice had gone, the emperor sat near the pool and gazed at the jade stone. The shining scales of the jade carp glowed in the moonlight. The fishes' slippery bodies were reflected in the pool. They seemed ready to flick their tails and swim among the reeds.

NARRATOR 3: The emperor remained by the pool until his advisers found him at sunrise.

ADVISER 3: What punishment have your dreams chosen?

EMPEROR: (smiling) Bring Chan Lo before me.

* * *

NARRATOR 1: Chan Lo bowed deeply before the Great Emperor of All China, ready to receive his terrible punishment.

EMPEROR: You have disobeyed me, Chan Lo, but you are a brave man to defy the Great Emperor of All China. You have carved the creatures that were in the stone. I, too, have heard them. These three carp fish are dearer to me than any dragon of wind and fire. What reward would you have?

CHAN LO: (grateful and relieved, bowing even lower) Great Emperor, your happiness with my work is my reward. I wish only to return to my village and carve what I hear.

EMPEROR: You *will* carve what you hear. And you will return to your village in great honor—as befits the Master Carver to the Great Emperor of All China!

STONE: Pah-*tah!*

Jumping Mouse

A Plains Indian teaching tale,
by Hyemeyohsts Storm

Adapted from *Seven Arrows*, Harper & Row, 1972

12–13 ROLES: Narrator 1, Narrator 2, Narrator 3, Narrator 4, Jumping Mouse, Mouse 1, Mouse 2, Raccoon, Frog, Old Mouse, Buffalo, Wolf, (Eagle)

12 minutes

NOTE: This is an original story by Hyemeyohsts Storm, written in the Plains Indian spiritual tradition. According to the author, words capitalized in this story are "words to which the Teacher would have given inflections . . . to reflect symbolic content." For a discussion of the tale's deeper meaning, see *Seven Arrows*.

NARRATOR 1: Among the Indian People of the Plains—the Cheyenne, the Crow, and the Sioux—Stories were used to Teach the meaning of the Sun Dance Way.

NARRATOR 4: These Stories were magical Teachers, Flowers of Truth whose petals could be unfolded without end by the Seeker.

NARRATOR 2: Come sit with us, and let us smoke the Pipe of Peace in Understanding. Let us, each to the other, be a Gift.

NARRATOR 3: Let us Teach each other here in this Great Lodge of the People, this Sun Dance, about the Ways on this Great Medicine Wheel, our Earth.

* * *

NARRATOR 1: Once there was a Mouse.

NARRATOR 4: He was a busy Mouse, searching everywhere, touching his whiskers to the grass and looking. He was busy as all Mice are—busy with Mice things.

NARRATOR 2: But once in a while he would hear an odd sound.

NARRATOR 3: He would lift his head, squinting hard to see, his whiskers wiggling in the air. And he would wonder.

NARRATOR 1: One day, he scurried up to a fellow Mouse and asked,

JUMPING: Do you hear a roaring, my Brother?

MOUSE 1: No, no.

NARRATOR 4: . . . answered the other Mouse, not lifting his busy nose from the ground.

MOUSE 1: I hear nothing. I am busy now. Talk to me later.

NARRATOR 2: He asked another Mouse.

JUMPING: Brother, do you hear a roaring sound?

MOUSE 2: Are you foolish in the head? *What* sound?

NARRATOR 3: And the Mouse slipped away.

NARRATOR 1: The little Mouse shrugged his whiskers and busied himself again.

NARRATOR 4: But again, there was that roaring.

NARRATOR 2: It was faint,

NARRATOR 3: but it was there!

NARRATOR 1: One day, he decided to investigate. He scurried a little way from the other busy Mice and listened again.

NARRATOR 4: There it was!

NARRATOR 2: He was listening hard when a voice made him jump.

RACCOON: Hello, little Brother. It is I, Brother Raccoon. What are you doing here all by yourself?

NARRATOR 3: The Mouse blushed and put his nose almost to the ground.

JUMPING: I hear a roaring, and I am investigating it.

RACCOON: A roaring? What you hear, little Brother, is the River!

JUMPING: The River? What is a River?

RACCOON: Walk with me and I will show you.

NARRATOR 1: Little Mouse walked with Raccoon along strange paths. Many times he was so frightened, he almost turned back.

NARRATOR 4: But he was determined to find out once and for all about the roaring.

NARRATOR 2: Finally they came to the River. It was huge and breathtaking.

NARRATOR 3: Little Mouse could not see across it, it was so great.

NARRATOR 1: It roared,

NARRATOR 4: sang,

NARRATOR 2: cried,

NARRATOR 3: and thundered.

JUMPING: It is powerful!

RACCOON: It is a Great Thing. I must leave you now, little Brother. But do not fear, for Frog will take care of you. *(leaves)*

FROG: Welcome to the River, little Brother.

NARRATOR 1: On a lily pad sat a Frog, almost as green as the pad it sat on.

JUMPING: Are you not afraid to be that far out into the Great River?

FROG: No, I am not afraid. I have been given the gift to live both above and within the River. I, my Brother, am the Keeper of the Water. Would you like some Medicine Power?

JUMPING: Medicine Power? Me? Yes, yes, if I could!

FROG: Then crouch as low as you can, and jump as high as you can.

NARRATOR 4: Little Mouse crouched as low as he could, and jumped.

NARRATOR 2: When he did, he saw the Sacred Mountains!

NARRATOR 3: He could hardly believe his eyes.

NARRATOR 1: But then he fell back and landed in the River!

NARRATOR 4: Little Mouse scrambled back to the bank. He was frightened nearly to death.

JUMPING: You tricked me!

FROG: Wait! You were not harmed. Do not let your fear and anger blind you. What did you see?

JUMPING: I . . . I saw the Sacred Mountains!

FROG: And you have a new name! It is . . . Jumping Mouse!

*   *   *

NARRATOR 1: Jumping Mouse returned to the world of the Mice. But no one would listen to what he told them. And many Mice were afraid of him, because he was wet and there had been no rain to explain it.

NARRATOR 4: The memory of the Sacred Mountains burned in the mind and heart of Jumping Mouse. One day, he went to the edge of the place of Mice and looked out onto the Prairie.

NARRATOR 2: The sky was full of many spots. Each spot was an Eagle that would eat a Mouse.

NARRATOR 3: But Jumping Mouse was determined to go to the Sacred Mountains. He gathered all his courage and ran as fast he could onto the Prairie.

NARRATOR 1: Jumping Mouse ran until he came to a stand of sage.

NARRATOR 4: He was catching his breath when he saw an old Mouse.

OLD MOUSE: Welcome!

NARRATOR 2: The patch of sage that Old Mouse lived in was a haven for Mice.

NARRATOR 3: Seeds were plentiful, and there were many things to be busy with.

JUMPING: This is truly a wonderful place! And the Eagles cannot see you here, either!

OLD MOUSE: Yes, and you can see all the Beings of the Prairie from here—Rabbit, Buffalo, Antelope, Coyote—and you can know their names.

JUMPING: Can you also see the River and the Great Mountains?

OLD MOUSE: I know there is the Great River. But I am afraid the Great Mountains are only a myth. Forget them and stay here with me. Everything you want is here!

JUMPING: Thank you, Old Mouse, but I must seek the Mountains.

OLD MOUSE: You are foolish to leave! There is danger on the Prairie. See all those spots up there? They are Eagles, and they will catch you!

NARRATOR 1: It was hard for Jumping Mouse to leave. But he gathered his determination and ran hard again. He could feel the shadows of the spots pass over his back.

NARRATOR 4: Finally, he ran into a stand of chokecherries. Here were many things to gather, and many busy things to do. He was investigating this new domain, when he heard heavy breathing.

NARRATOR 2: Beside the chokecherry stand lay a great Buffalo!

NARRATOR 3: He was so large, Jumping Mouse could have crawled into one of his horns.

BUFFALO: Hello, my Brother. Thank you for visiting me.

JUMPING: Hello, Great Being. Why are you lying here?

BUFFALO: I am sick and dying. My Medicine has told me I can be healed only by the eye of a Mouse. But there is no such thing as a Mouse!

NARRATOR 1: Jumping Mouse was shocked. He scurried back into the stand of chokecherries.

NARRATOR 4: But the Buffalo's breathing came harder and slower.

JUMPING: He will die if I do not give him one of my eyes. He is too great a Being to let die!

NARRATOR 2: He went back to the Buffalo.

JUMPING: *I* am a Mouse. I have two eyes, so you may have one of them.

NARRATOR 3: The moment he said it, Jumping Mouse's eye flew from his head, and the Buffalo was made whole.

JUMPING: *(covers one eye with hand)*

NARRATOR 1: The Buffalo jumped to his feet.

BUFFALO: Thank you, little Brother! You have given me life, so I may give of myself to the People. I know of your quest for the Sacred Mountains. Run under my belly, and I will take you right to their foot. You need not fear the Eagles, for they will see only the back of a Buffalo.

NARRATOR 4: Jumping Mouse ran under the Buffalo, secure and hidden.

NARRATOR 2: But with only one eye, it was frightening. The Buffalo's great hooves shook the whole world.

NARRATOR 3: Finally, the Buffalo stopped.

BUFFALO: This is where I must leave you, little Brother. I am of the Prairie, and I will fall on you if I try to go up the Mountains.

JUMPING: Thank you. But you know, it was very frightening running under you with only one eye.

BUFFALO: Your fear was for nothing, for my way of walking is the Sun Dance Way. I always know where my hooves will fall. *(leaves)*

NARRATOR 1: Jumping Mouse investigated this new place. There were even more things here than in the other places—busier things, things that Mice like.

NARRATOR 4: Suddenly he ran upon a gray Wolf, sitting there doing nothing.

JUMPING: Hello, Brother Wolf.

NARRATOR 2: The Wolf's ears pricked up, and his eyes shone.

WOLF: Wolf? Wolf? Yes, that is what I am! A Wolf!

NARRATOR 3: But his eyes dimmed again, and he sat quietly once more.

JUMPING: Brother Wolf?

WOLF: Wolf? Yes, that's it! I'm a Wolf!

NARRATOR 1: But again he grew still.

JUMPING: Such a Great Being. But he has no memory!

NARRATOR 4: Jumping Mouse listened for a long time to the beating of his heart. Then suddenly he made up his mind.

JUMPING: Brother Wolf—

WOLF: Wolf? Wolf?

JUMPING: Brother Wolf, please listen to me! I know what will heal you. It is one of my eyes. You are a greater Being than I. Please take it.

NARRATOR 2: The eye of Jumping Mouse flew from his head, and the Wolf was made whole.

JUMPING: (covers both eyes with hand)

NARRATOR 3: Tears fell down the cheeks of Wolf, but Jumping Mouse could not see them, for now he was blind.

WOLF: You are a Great Brother, for now I have my memory! I am the Guide into the Sacred Mountains. There is a Great Medicine Lake there, the most beautiful lake in the world.

JUMPING: Please take me there!

NARRATOR 1: The Wolf guided him through the pines to the Medicine Lake.

NARRATOR 4: Jumping Mouse drank its water as the Wolf described its beauty.

WOLF: All the world is reflected in the lake: the People, the Lodges of the People, and all the Beings of the Prairies and Skies. But now I must leave you, for I must return to guide others. (leaves)

NARRATOR 2: Jumping Mouse sat trembling in fear.

NARRATOR 3: He knew an Eagle would find him here. But it was no use running, for he was blind.

NARRATOR 1: He felt a shadow on his back.

NARRATOR 4: He heard the sound that Eagles make.

NARRATOR 2: The Eagle hit!

NARRATOR 3: Jumping Mouse went to sleep.

*   *   *

NARRATOR 1: Then Jumping Mouse . . . woke up!

NARRATOR 4: How surprised he was to be alive! But there was another surprise as well.

JUMPING: I can see! I can see!

NARRATOR 2: Everything was blurry, but the colors were beautiful!

NARRATOR 3: Just then, a blurred shape came toward Jumping Mouse.

FROG: Hello, Brother! Do you want some Medicine?

JUMPING: Some Medicine, for me? Yes, yes!

FROG: Then crouch as low as you can, and jump as high as you can.

NARRATOR 1: Jumping Mouse crouched as low as he could, and jumped.

NARRATOR 4: The Wind caught him and carried him higher.

FROG: Do not be afraid! Hang on to the Wind, and trust!

NARRATOR 2: Jumping Mouse closed his eyes and hung on to the Wind, and it carried him higher and higher.

NARRATOR 3: Then Jumping Mouse opened his eyes, and they were clear, and the higher he went, the clearer they became.

NARRATOR 1: Down on the Medicine Lake, sitting on a lily pad, he saw his old friend, Frog.

FROG: (calling up) You have a new name! You are . . . Eagle!

Three Sideways Stories

By Louis Sachar

From *Sideways Stories from Wayside School*, Avon, 1985

9 ROLES: Narrator 1, Narrator 2, Narrator 3, Narrator 4, Mrs. Jewls, Joe, Bebe, Calvin, Louis

12 minutes

NARRATOR 1: We're going to tell you about three of the children in Mrs. Jewls's class, on the thirtieth story of Wayside School.

NARRATOR 4: But before we get to them, there is something you ought to know. Wayside School was accidentally built *sideways*.

NARRATOR 2: It was supposed to be only one story high, with thirty classrooms all in a row. Instead, it is *thirty* stories high, with one classroom on each *story*.

NARRATOR 3: The builder said he was very sorry.

* * *

NARRATOR 1: Our first story is about Joe. One day, Mrs. Jewls kept him in from recess.

MRS. JEWLS: Joe, you are going to have to learn to count.

JOE: But, Mrs. Jewls, I already *know* how to count. Let me go to recess!

MRS. JEWLS: First count to ten.

NARRATOR 4: Joe counted to ten.

JOE: Six, eight, twelve, one, five, two, seven, eleven, three, ten.

MRS. JEWLS: No, Joe, that is wrong.

JOE: No, it isn't! I counted until I got to ten!

MRS. JEWLS: But you were *wrong*. I'll *prove* it to you.

NARRATOR 2: She put down five pencils.

MRS. JEWLS: How many pencils do we have here, Joe?

NARRATOR 3: Joe counted the pencils.

JOE: Four, six, one, nine, five. There are five pencils, Mrs. Jewls.

MRS. JEWLS: That's *wrong*.

JOE: How many pencils *are* there?

MRS. JEWLS: Five.

JOE: That's what I said! May I go to recess now?

MRS. JEWLS: No. You got the right answer, but you counted the wrong *way*. You were just lucky.

NARRATOR 1: She set down eight potatoes.

MRS. JEWLS: How many potatoes, Joe?

NARRATOR 4: Joe counted the potatoes.

JOE: Seven, five, three, one, two, four, six, eight. There are eight potatoes, Mrs. Jewls.

MRS. JEWLS: No, there are *eight*.

JOE: But that's what I said! May I go to recess now?

MRS. JEWLS: No! You got the right answer, but you counted the wrong *way* again.

NARRATOR 2: She put down three books.

MRS. JEWLS: Count the books, Joe.

NARRATOR 3: Joe counted the books.

JOE: A thousand, a million, three. Three, Mrs. Jewls.

MRS. JEWLS: *(bewildered)* Correct.

JOE: May I go to recess now?

MRS. JEWLS: No.

JOE: May I have a potato?

MRS. JEWLS: No! *Listen* to me. One, two, three, four, five, six, seven, eight, nine, ten. Now *you* say it.

JOE: One, two, three, four, five, six, seven, eight, nine, ten.

MRS. JEWLS: Very good!

NARRATOR 1: She put down six erasers.

MRS. JEWLS: Now, count the erasers, Joe, just the way I showed you.

NARRATOR 4: Joe counted the erasers.

JOE: One, two, three, four, five, six, seven, eight, nine, ten. There are ten, Mrs. Jewls.

MRS. JEWLS: No!

JOE: Didn't I count right?

MRS. JEWLS: Yes, you *counted* right, but you got the wrong *answer*.

JOE: This doesn't make any sense! When I count the *wrong* way, I get the *right* answer, and when I count *right*, I get the *wrong* answer.

MRS. JEWLS: *(in great frustration)* Ooh!

NARRATOR 2: Mrs. Jewls hit her head against the wall five times.

MRS. JEWLS: How many times did I hit my head against the wall, Joe?

JOE: One, two, three, four, five, six, seven, eight, nine, ten. You hit your head against the wall ten times.

MRS. JEWLS: No!

JOE: Four, six, one, nine, five. You hit your head five times.

NARRATOR 3: Mrs. Jewls shook her head no and said,

MRS. JEWLS: *(shaking head)* Yes, that is right.

NARRATOR 1: Just then, the bell rang.

JOE: Oh, darn.

NARRATOR 4: . . . said Joe.

JOE: I missed recess!

*   *   *

NARRATOR 3: Our second story is about Bebe.

NARRATOR 1: Bebe was the fastest draw in Mrs. Jewls's class. She could draw a cat in less than forty-five seconds, a dog in less than thirty, and a flower in less than eight seconds!

NARRATOR 4: But of course, Bebe never drew just *one* dog, or *one* cat, or *one* flower.

NARRATOR 2: Art was from twelve-thirty to one-thirty. Why, in that time, she could draw fifty cats, a hundred flowers, twenty dogs, and several eggs or watermelons!

NARRATOR 3: You see, it took her the same time to draw a watermelon as an egg.

NARRATOR 1: Calvin sat next to Bebe. He didn't think he was very good at art. It took him the whole period just to draw one airplane.

NARRATOR 4: So instead, he just helped Bebe. He was Bebe's assistant.

NARRATOR 2: As soon as Bebe would finish one masterpiece, Calvin would take it from her and set down a clean sheet of paper. Whenever her crayon ran low, Calvin was ready with a new crayon.

NARRATOR 3: That way, Bebe didn't have to waste any time. And in return, Bebe would draw five or six airplanes for Calvin.

NARRATOR 1: It was twelve-thirty, time for art.

NARRATOR 4: Bebe was ready. On her desk was a sheet of yellow construction paper. In her hand was a green crayon.

NARRATOR 2: *Calvin* was ready. He held a stack of paper and a box of crayons.

CALVIN: Ready, Bebe?

BEBE: Ready, Calvin.

MRS. JEWLS: All right, class.

NARRATOR 3: . . . said Mrs. Jewls.

MRS. JEWLS: Time for art.

NARRATOR 1: She had hardly finished her sentence when Bebe had drawn a picture of a leaf.

NARRATOR 4: Calvin took it from her and put down another piece of paper.

BEBE: Red!

NARRATOR 2: Calvin handed Bebe a red crayon.

BEBE: Blue!

NARRATOR 3: He gave her a blue crayon.

NARRATOR 1: They were quite a pair! Their teamwork was remarkable.

NARRATOR 4: Bebe drew pictures as fast as Calvin could pick up the old paper and set down the new.

NARRATOR 2: A fish.

NARRATOR 3: An apple.

NARRATOR 1: Three cherries—

NARRATOR 4: *bing,*

NARRATOR 2: *bing,*

NARRATOR 3: *bing.*

NARRATOR 1: At one-thirty, Mrs. Jewls announced,

MRS. JEWLS: Okay, class, art is over.

NARRATOR 4: Bebe dropped her crayon and fell over on her desk.

NARRATOR 2: Calvin sighed and leaned back in his chair. He could hardly move.

NARRATOR 3: They had broken their old record. Bebe had drawn three hundred and seventy-eight pictures! They lay in a pile on Calvin's desk.

NARRATOR 1: Mrs. Jewls walked by.

MRS. JEWLS: Calvin, did you draw all these pictures?

CALVIN: No, *Bebe* drew them all.

MRS. JEWLS: Well, then, what did *you* draw?

CALVIN: I didn't draw anything.

MRS. JEWLS: Why not? Don't you like art?

CALVIN: I *love* art. That's why I didn't draw anything.

MRS. JEWLS: I don't understand.

CALVIN: It would have taken me the whole period just to draw one picture. And *Bebe* would only have been able to draw a *hundred* pictures. But with the two of us working together, she was able to draw three hundred and seventy-eight pictures! That's a lot more art.

NARRATOR 4: Bebe and Calvin shook hands.

MRS. JEWLS: No, no! *That* isn't how you measure art. It isn't how *many* pictures you have, but how good the pictures *are*. Why, a person could spend their whole life drawing just one picture of a cat. In that time, I'm sure Bebe could draw a *million* cats.

BEBE: *Two* million.

MRS. JEWLS: But if that one picture is better than each of Bebe's two million, then that person has produced more art than Bebe.

NARRATOR 2: Bebe looked like she was going to cry. She picked up all the pictures from Calvin's desk and threw them in the garbage.

NARRATOR 3: Then she ran from the room, down all the stairs, and out onto the playground.

NARRATOR 1: Louis, the nice yard teacher, spotted her.

LOUIS: Where are you going, Bebe?

BEBE: I'm going home to draw a picture of a cat.

LOUIS: Will you bring it to school and show it to me tomorrow?

BEBE: *Tomorrow?* By *tomorrow* I doubt I'll be finished with even one *whisker*. (*rushes off*)

* * *

NARRATOR 2: Our final story is about Calvin. One day, Mrs. Jewls said,

MRS. JEWLS: Calvin, I want you to take this note to Miss Zarves for me.

CALVIN: Miss Zarves?

MRS. JEWLS: Yes, Miss Zarves. You know where she is, don't you?

CALVIN: Yes. She's on the nineteenth story.

MRS. JEWLS: That's right, Calvin. Take it to her.

NARRATOR 3: Calvin didn't move.

MRS. JEWLS: Well, what are you waiting for?

CALVIN: She's on the nineteenth story.

MRS. JEWLS: Yes, we have already established that fact.

CALVIN: The *nineteenth story*.

MRS. JEWLS: Yes, Calvin, the *nineteenth story*. Now take it to her before I lose my patience!

CALVIN: But, Mrs. Jewls—

MRS. JEWLS: NOW, Calvin!

CALVIN: Yes, ma'am!

NARRATOR 1: Calvin walked out of the classroom and stood outside the door.

NARRATOR 4: He didn't know where to go.

NARRATOR 2: As you know, when the builder built Wayside School, he accidentally built it sideways. But he *also* forgot to build the nineteenth *story*.

NARRATOR 3: He built the eighteenth and the twentieth, but no nineteenth. He said he was very sorry.

NARRATOR 1: There was also no Miss Zarves.

NARRATOR 4: Miss Zarves taught the class on the nineteenth story. Since there was no nineteenth story, there was no Miss Zarves.

NARRATOR 2: And besides *that,* as if Calvin didn't have enough problems, there was no note.

NARRATOR 3: Mrs. Jewls had never given Calvin the note.

CALVIN: (*sarcastically*) Boy, this is just great! I'm supposed to take a note that I don't have, to a teacher who doesn't exist, and who teaches on a story that was never built!

NARRATOR 1: He didn't know what to do.

NARRATOR 4: He walked down to the eighteenth story,

NARRATOR 2: then back up to the twentieth,

NARRATOR 3: then back down to the eighteenth,

NARRATOR 1: and back up again to the twentieth.

NARRATOR 4: There was no nineteenth story.

NARRATOR 2: There had never *been* a nineteenth story.

NARRATOR 3: There would never BE a nineteenth story.

NARRATOR 1: Calvin walked down to the administration office on the first story. He decided to put the note in Miss Zarves's mailbox.

NARRATOR 4: But there wasn't one of those, either. That didn't bother Calvin too much, though, since he didn't have a note.

NARRATOR 2: He looked out the window and saw Louis, the yard teacher, shooting baskets.

CALVIN: *Louis* will know what to do.

NARRATOR 3: Calvin went outside.

CALVIN: Hey, Louis!

LOUIS: Hi, Calvin. Do you want to play a game?

CALVIN: I don't have time. I have to deliver a note to Miss Zarves up on the nineteenth story.

LOUIS: Then what are you doing all the way down here?

CALVIN: There is no nineteenth story.

LOUIS: Then where is Miss Zarves?

CALVIN: There is no Miss Zarves.

LOUIS: What are you going to do with the note?

CALVIN: There is no note.

LOUIS: I understand.

CALVIN: That's good, because *I* sure don't.

LOUIS: It's very simple. You are not supposed to take no notes to no teachers. You already haven't done it!

NARRATOR 1: Calvin still didn't understand.

CALVIN: I'll just have to tell Mrs. Jewls that I couldn't deliver the note.

LOUIS: *That's* good. The truth is always best. Besides, I don't think *I* understand what I said, either!

NARRATOR 4: Calvin walked back up the thirty flights of stairs to Mrs. Jewls's class.

MRS. JEWLS: Thank you very much, Calvin.

CALVIN: But I—

MRS. JEWLS: That was a very important note, and I'm glad I was able to count on you.

CALVIN: Yes, but you see—

MRS. JEWLS: The note was very important. I told Miss Zarves *not* to meet me for lunch.

CALVIN: Don't worry.

NARRATOR 2: . . . said Calvin.

CALVIN: She won't!

* * *

NARRATOR 1: So now you know about Wayside School. Some people say these stories are strange and silly.

NARRATOR 4: That is probably true.

NARRATOR 2: But when the children at Wayside School heard stories about *us*, they thought *we* were strange and silly.

NARRATOR 3: And *that's* for *sure!*

The Bean Boy

By Monica Shannon

From *California Fairy Tales*, Doubleday, 1927

8 ROLES: Narrator 1, Narrator 2, Narrator 3, Narrator 4, Bean Boy, Dulce, Goblin/Governor, Sandman/Soldier

8 minutes

NOTE: In this original "California fairy tale," Monica Shannon draws both on the Mexican colonial heritage of California, and on her own Irish heritage.

NARRATOR 1: In the years between this and that, there lived a little boy named String,

NARRATOR 4: because he used strings for shoelaces—

BEAN BOY: (*pointing to each shoe*) A red string in one shoe, and a green string in the other.

NARRATOR 2: Now, String lived in a lima bean field. And when the lima beans were green, he picked them, put them in sacks, and took sackfuls of green lima beans into town to sell.

NARRATOR 3: So he was called the Bean Boy.

NARRATOR 1: One morning, String the Bean Boy started off for the governor's palace with a sack of green lima beans. The governor's little daughter had ordered large, flat beans for her soup.

NARRATOR 4: She was called Dulce because, although her eyes were dark and sad, her smile was as sweet and gaudy as the red seaweed, dulce.

NARRATOR 2: Now, Dulce was leaning out of the palace window, watching for her sack of large, flat beans. The Bean Boy came whistling into the patio of the palace, tripping over his shoestrings—

BEAN BOY: (*trips, then points*) A red string, and a green string.

NARRATOR 2: always coming undone.

NARRATOR 3: Dulce ran downstairs, fetching a pan, so the Bean Boy could dump out his sack of big, flat beans. Then the Bean Boy sat down to tie up his green and red shoestrings.

NARRATOR 1: By this time, the governor's little daughter had stopped smiling, so String noticed how sad and dark her eyes looked. The little girl said,

DULCE: It must be nice to live in a Bean Field and bring sacks of beans into town.

BEAN BOY: It *is* nice. And I am always finding things on my way in and out.

DULCE: What *kind* of things?

BEAN BOY: Oh, tree toads, and moonstones, and old Spanish coins, and Indian beads, and kelp for dress-up helmets!

NARRATOR 4: The governor's little daughter smiled her gaudy smile.

DULCE: Maybe . . . maybe you can find my dream for me?

BEAN BOY: Maybe I can!

DULCE: I dreamed that my father was not a governor any more, and he didn't need to worry about revolutions. I dreamed he was an organ-grinder man, with a tiny tomboy monkey from Central America.

BEAN BOY: (*encouragingly*) I know. And you went with him, walking through bean fields, singing "Ma-*ri*-a *Mi*-a." And people filled your cup with pennies. And you made a bonfire every night and popped corn.

DULCE: Yes! Yes! And my father didn't worry any more about revolutions. Just think, he didn't need to worry about revolutions!

NARRATOR 2: Dulce opened her sad eyes wide open.

DULCE: But I only dreamed it once. Now, do you think you can find my dream again for me?

BEAN BOY: Of course! I can find *anything* on my way in and out.

DULCE: Then I mean to marry you when you grow up tall!

NARRATOR 3: At that, the Bean Boy went whistling away, tripping over his shoestrings—

BEAN BOY: (*trips and points*) A red string, and a green string. (*goes off whistling*)

NARRATOR 3: always coming undone.

* * *

NARRATOR 1: Next morning at sun up, String the Bean Boy was picking big, flat beans and putting them into sacks, when a Goblin came hurrying up a bean row. The Goblin tipped his bean-leaf cap and inquired politely,

GOBLIN: Could you possibly spare two good-sized beans this morning? The finest baby of our king will be christened in sixteen minutes, and I find myself without a christening present.

NARRATOR 4: The polite Goblin bowed as best he could, for he was a thick little person. He had a wide, cheerful mouth, and looked hearty in his seaweed suit.

BEAN BOY: Fill your cap!

NARRATOR 2: . . . String told him, and he helped the Goblin pick eight or ten fine lima beans. Then he said in a hurry,

BEAN BOY: While you are here, I wish you would tell me where to find the dream of the governor's little girl, Dulce.

GOBLIN: (*bows*) Certainly. All dreams are kept in the Cave of Yawns, down by the sea—two leagues south, two leagues west. But remember not to yawn in the cave! Every time anyone yawns, the cave gets bigger. And if you go to sleep in there, you will never wake up.

NARRATOR 3: Then the Goblin hurried off to the king's baby's christening.

NARRATOR 1: The Bean Boy hurried off too, going two leagues south, two leagues west.

NARRATOR 4: And there he was, down by the sea, at the Cave of Yawns.

NARRATOR 2: There were dark chests along the cave walls—rich, hand-carved chests, from which the Sandman was selecting dreams.

NARRATOR 3: The Sandman stood at the farthest end of the cave, throwing a handful of sand into his bag and then a dream, a handful of sand and then a dream.

NARRATOR 1: The Bean Boy called out,

BEAN BOY: Sandman!

NARRATOR 4: But when the Sandman looked up, the Bean Boy yawned. The cave got bigger, just as the polite Goblin had said it would. The Sandman was leagues farther away now.

NARRATOR 2: The Bean Boy began to feel sleepy.

NARRATOR 3: His hands went to sleep, his feet went to sleep, and every step pricked like pins and needles.

NARRATOR 1: Then the Bean Boy yawned again, and the cave got bigger, just as the polite Goblin had said it would. The Sandman and the rich, hand-carved chests were so far away now, they looked like dots on a dotted line.

NARRATOR 4: Then the Bean Boy's ears went to sleep. After that, his nose went to sleep. But he said to himself,

BEAN BOY: Even though I feel all over like a pincushion, I must keep my two eyes awake and walk with my feet asleep, until I can nudge the Sandman and get Dulce's dream for her.

NARRATOR 2: So the Bean Boy walked with his feet asleep, his hands asleep, his ears asleep, and his nose asleep. But the jolt of tripping over his shoestrings kept his eyes awake, until he nudged the Sandman.

NARRATOR 3: The Bean Boy stifled an enormous yawn.

BEAN BOY: (making faces, talking slow and funny, as he struggles not to yawn) Please, may I have Dulce's dream?

SANDMAN: What was it like? And about how long?

BEAN BOY: Hurry! I'm going to yawn again!

SANDMAN: (searching in a chest) Did it have a monkey and an organ grinder in it? And a song that goes, "Ma-ri-a Mi-a?"

BEAN BOY: (still struggling) Yes! Yes!

NARRATOR 1: The Bean Boy's eyes were closing. But he tripped over his shoestrings and opened his eyes again with a terrible effort.

SANDMAN: (holds the dream up like a piece of clothing, looks it up and down) It's an old dream, almost worn out. So I suppose you may as well have it.

NARRATOR 4: The Sandman shook the dream out, sticking his finger through the holes. Then he handed over the tattered dream.

NARRATOR 2: The Bean Boy ran from the cave with his feet asleep, his hands asleep, his ears asleep, and his nose asleep.

NARRATOR 3: He was really asleep all over, except that his eyes were awake from the jolt of tripping over his shoestrings—

BEAN BOY: (trips and points, still struggling not to yawn) a red string in one shoe . . . and a green string in the other. (runs off)

*   *   *

NARRATOR 1: Next morning before dawn, the little boy started for town with his bean sacks and the old dream, which looked as if it were falling to pieces.

NARRATOR 4: When he came near the gates of the town, he heard guns! Soldiers came out, singing,

NARRATORS 1, 2, 3, 4: Ma-ri-a Mi-a!

NARRATOR 1: The Bean Boy went into town. The palace was in ruins, and there on some stones sat the governor and Dulce. The Bean Boy noticed how sad and dark her eyes were.

GOVERNOR: It is just what I worried about!

NARRATOR 4: . . . moaned the governor. And Dulce told the Bean Boy,

DULCE: We have had another revolution.

NARRATOR 2: Just then, a soldier came running up and spoke low to the governor.

SOLDIER: Your Excellency must go away at once in disguise!

GOVERNOR: (hopelessly) Where can I go? What can I do?

NARRATOR 3: Whereupon the Bean Boy handed him the old, worn dream.

GOVERNOR: (puts on dream and becomes organ-grinder)

*　*　*

NARRATOR 1: And so it happened that the governor disguised himself as an organ-grinder man, owning a tiny tomboy monkey from Central America.

NARRATOR 4: He and Dulce and String the Bean Boy wandered up and down the world joyously, making bonfires every night and popping corn.

NARRATOR 2: After they had wandered from one end of the world to the other, the Bean Boy married Dulce one night by a big campfire,

NARRATOR 3: and they inherited great stretches of bean fields,

NARRATOR 1: where they lived happily,

NARRATOR 4: for years,

NARRATOR 2: and years,

NARRATOR 3: and years,

BEAN BOY & DULCE: and years.

Savitri

A tale of ancient India, retold by Aaron Shepard

Adapted from *Savitri: A Tale of Ancient India,* Whitman, 1992

10 ROLES: Narrator 1, Narrator 2, Savitri, Satyavan, King 1, King 2, Teacher, Narada, Yama, Goddess

10 minutes

NOTE: This story is probably around 3000 years old. It was first written down about 2000 years ago as part of the *Mahabharata,* India's great national epic. *Savitri* is pronounced "SAH-vi-tree." *Satyavan* is pronounced "SOT-yuh-von." *Narada* is pronounced "NAH-ruh-duh." *Yama* is pronounced "YAH-muh." *Mahabharata* is pronounced "MAH-hah-BAH-ruh-tuh."

NARRATOR 1: In India, in the time of legend, there lived a king with many wives but not one child. Morning and evening for eighteen years, he faced the fire on the sacred altar and prayed for the gift of children.

NARRATOR 2: Finally, a shining goddess rose from the flames.

GODDESS: I am Savitri, child of the Sun. By your prayers, you have won a daughter.

NARRATOR 1: Within a year, a daughter came to the king and his favorite wife. He named her Savitri, after the goddess.

NARRATOR 2: Beauty and intelligence were the princess Savitri's, and eyes that shone like the sun. So splendid was she, people thought she herself was a goddess. Yet when the time came for her to marry, no man asked for her. Her father told her,

KING 1: Weak men turn away from radiance like yours. Go out and find a man worthy of you. Then I will arrange the marriage.

NARRATOR 1: In the company of servants and councilors, Savitri traveled from place to place. After many days, she came upon a hermitage by a river crossing. Here lived many who had left the towns and cities for a life of prayer and study.

NARRATOR 2: Savitri entered the hall of worship and bowed to the eldest teacher. As they spoke, a young man with shining eyes came into the hall. He guided another man, old and blind.

SAVITRI: *(softly, to the teacher)* Who is that young man?

TEACHER: *(smiling)* That is Prince Satyavan. He guides his father, a king whose realm was conquered. It is well that Satyavan's name means "Son of Truth," for no man is richer in virtue.

NARRATOR 1: When Savitri returned home, she found her father with the holy seer called Narada.

KING 1: Daughter, have you found a man you wish to marry?

SAVITRI: Yes, father. His name is Satyavan.

NARADA: *(gasps)* Not Satyavan! Princess, no man could be more worthy, but you must not marry him! I know the future. Satyavan will die, one year from today!

KING 1: Do you hear, daughter? Choose a different husband!

NARRATOR 2: Savitri trembled but said,

SAVITRI: I have chosen Satyavan, and I will not choose another. However long or short his life, I wish to share it.

NARRATOR 1: Soon the king went with Savitri to arrange the marriage.

NARRATOR 2: Satyavan was overjoyed to be offered such a bride. But his father, the blind king, asked Savitri,

KING 2: Can you bear the hard life of the hermitage? Will you wear our simple robe, and our coat of matted bark? Will you eat only fruit and plants of the wild?

SAVITRI: I care nothing about comfort or hardship. In palace or in hermitage, I am content.

NARRATOR 1: That very day, Savitri and Satyavan walked hand in hand around the sacred fire in the hall of worship.

NARRATOR 2: In front of all the priests and hermits, they became husband and wife.

* * *

NARRATOR 1: For a year, they lived happily. But Savitri could never forget that Satyavan's death drew closer.

NARRATOR 2: Finally, only three days remained. Savitri entered the hall of worship and faced the sacred fire. There she prayed for three days and nights, not eating or sleeping.

SATYAVAN: My love, prayer and fasting are good. But why be this hard on yourself?

NARRATOR 2: Savitri gave no answer.

NARRATOR 1: The sun was just rising when Savitri at last left the hall. She saw Satyavan heading for the forest, an ax on his shoulder.

NARRATOR 2: Savitri rushed to his side.

SAVITRI: I will come with you.

SATYAVAN: Stay here, my love. You should eat and rest.

SAVITRI: My heart is set on going.

NARRATOR 1: Hand in hand, Savitri and Satyavan walked over wooded hills. They smelled the blossoms on flowering trees, and paused beside clear streams. The cries of peacocks echoed through the woods.

NARRATOR 2: While Savitri rested, Satyavan chopped firewood from a fallen tree. Suddenly, he dropped his ax.

SATYAVAN: My head aches.

NARRATOR 1: Savitri rushed to him. She set him down in the shade of a tree.

SATYAVAN: My body is burning! What is wrong with me?

NARRATOR 2: Satyavan's eyes closed. His breathing slowed.

NARRATOR 1: Savitri looked up. Coming through the woods to meet them was a princely man. He shone, though his skin was darker than the darkest night. His eyes and his robe were the red of blood. Trembling, Savitri asked,

SAVITRI: Who *are* you?

YAMA: *(gently)* Princess, you see me only by the power of your prayer and fasting. I am Yama, god of death. Now is the time I must take the spirit of Satyavan.

NARRATOR 2: Yama took a small noose and passed it through Satyavan's breast, as if through air. He drew out a tiny likeness of Satyavan, no bigger than a thumb. Satyavan's breathing stopped.

YAMA: Happiness awaits your husband in my kingdom. Satyavan is a man of great virtue.

NARRATOR 1: Yama placed the likeness inside his robe. Then he turned and headed south, back to his domain.

NARRATOR 2: Savitri rose and started after him.

NARRATOR 1: Yama strode smoothly and swiftly through the woods, while Savitri struggled to keep up. Finally, Yama turned to face her.

YAMA: Savitri! You cannot follow to the land of the dead!

SAVITRI: Lord Yama, I know your duty is to take my husband. But my duty as his wife is to stay beside him!

YAMA: Princess, that duty is at an end! Still, I admire your loyalty. I will grant you a favor—anything but the life of your husband.

SAVITRI: Please restore my father-in-law's kingdom and his sight.

YAMA: His sight and his kingdom shall be restored.

NARRATOR 2: Yama again headed south.

NARRATOR 1: Savitri followed.

NARRATOR 2: Along a riverbank, thorns and tall sharp grass let Yama pass untouched. But they tore at Savitri's clothes and skin.

YAMA: Savitri! You have come far enough!

SAVITRI: Lord Yama, I know my husband will find happiness in your kingdom. But you carry away the happiness that is mine!

YAMA: Princess, even love must bend to fate! Still, I admire your devotion. I will grant you another favor—anything but the life of your husband.

SAVITRI: Grant many more children to my father.

YAMA: Your father shall have many more children.

NARRATOR 1: Yama once more turned south.

NARRATOR 2: Again, Savitri followed.

NARRATOR 1: Up a steep hill Yama glided, while Savitri clambered after. At the top, Yama halted.

YAMA: Savitri! I forbid you to come farther!

SAVITRI: Lord Yama, you are respected and revered by all. Yet no matter what may come, I will remain by Satyavan!

YAMA: Princess, I tell you for the last time, you will not! Still, I can only admire your courage and your firmness. I will grant you one last favor— *anything* but the life of your husband!

SAVITRI: Then grant many children to *me*. And let them be children of Satyavan!

NARRATOR 2: Yama's eyes grew wide as he stared at Savitri.

YAMA: You did not ask for your husband's life, yet I cannot grant your wish without releasing him. Princess! Your wit is as strong as your will.

NARRATOR 1: Yama took out the spirit of Satyavan and removed the noose.

NARRATOR 2: The spirit flew north, quickly vanishing from sight.

YAMA: Return, Savitri. You have won your husband's life. *(leaves)*

NARRATOR 1: The sun was just setting when Savitri made her way back to Satyavan.

NARRATOR 2: His chest rose and fell. His eyes opened.

SATYAVAN: Is the day already gone? I have slept long. But what is wrong, my love? You smile and cry at the same time!

SAVITRI: My love, let us return home.

* * *

NARRATOR 1: Yama was true to all he had promised. Savitri's father became father to many more. Satyavan's father regained both sight and kingdom.

NARRATOR 2: In time, Satyavan became king, and Savitri his queen. They lived long and happily, blessed with many children. So they had no fear or tears when Yama came again to carry them to his kingdom.

The Flame of Peace

By Deborah Nourse Lattimore

Adapted from *The Flame of Peace*, Harper & Row, 1987

15–16+ ROLES: Narrator 1, Narrator 2, Two Flint, Emperor, Five Eagle, One Flower, Morning Star, Crossroads, River, Wind, (Storm), Earthquake, Volcano, Smoking Mirror, Lord Death, Lady Death, (People, Warriors, Ambassadors)

10 minutes

NOTE: This is an original story based on Aztec traditions. *Tenochtitlan* is pronounced "Tay-nawch-TEE-tlon." *Tezozomoc* is pronounced "Tay-zo-ZO-moc." *Itzcoatl* is pronounced "Its-co-AH-tul."

NARRATOR 1: Once, a great, long time ago, the capital of the Valley of Mexico had another name. It was called Tenochtitlan, Land of the Aztecs. Bustling marketplaces brimmed with people. Merchants traded in the sunny plazas. In gleaming temples, priests made offerings.

NARRATOR 2: There was a boy called Two Flint, who fished in the sparkling lake outside the city walls. Two Flint knew of no better place on earth.

NARRATOR 1: One day, Two Flint saw battle flags fluttering on the towers. Warriors stood along the walls. Emperor Itzcoatl himself appeared before the temple, draped in his imperial robes, and spoke to the people.

EMPEROR: Tezozomoc and his army are in the hills. He plans to capture our city. We must prepare ourselves. We will send ambassadors with gifts. Then we will see what kind of enemies these men are!

NARRATOR 2: Five Eagle, Two Flint's father, went to the marketplace to count the gifts for Tezozomoc. Two Flint asked him,

TWO FLINT: Why do we send gifts to our enemies?

FIVE EAGLE: For the Twenty Days of Talking. We will show Tezozomoc how great we are, by sending him our best things.

TWO FLINT: Will there be peace after the Twenty Days?

FIVE EAGLE: Maybe peace. Maybe war. Who knows? We have been enemies for many years.

NARRATOR 1: The next morning, Five Eagle stood before the temple with the other ambassadors. Priestesses danced before the stairs, as smoke curled up from incense burners. Conch shells sounded from tower to tower.

NARRATOR 2: The Emperor raised his arms. The ambassadors gave a salute.

NARRATOR 1: Five Eagle turned to his son.

FIVE EAGLE: Two Flint, one day *you* may have to search for peace. Be brave when that day comes!

NARRATOR 2: Then he marched from the city.

*   *   *

NARRATOR 1: For twenty days and twenty nights, Two Flint climbed the towers and squinted at the road leading to the hills.

NARRATOR 2: At last, ragged and limping figures appeared.

NARRATOR 1: But the father of Two Flint was not among them. Tezozomoc's warriors had taken his life.

EMPEROR: Let us prepare for war! Tezozomoc has broken the Twenty Days of Talking!

NARRATOR 2: The Emperor spilled copal juice down his face and arm.

EMPEROR: Tomorrow we face our enemy!

NARRATOR 1: Later, at home, Two Flint and his mother, One Flower, talked sadly.

TWO FLINT: Did we always fight the people from the shores of Lake Texcoco?

ONE FLOWER: Oh, no. Once, the sacred light of the Morning Star burned in our temples, and we were all brothers and sisters. But now the fire is dying. With no New Fire from Lord Morning Star, there can be no peace—only war.

TWO FLINT: Where is Lord Morning Star?

ONE FLOWER: There is a long road beyond the great city walls, ruled by nine evil demons of darkness. At the end of the road is the Hill of the Star. That is where they say Lord Morning Star can be found. But all who have ever searched for him were lost.

NARRATOR 2: The night, like a burning obsidian bowl, glowed with the flickering torches of foot runners, as the city prepared for war.

NARRATOR 1: Temple altars blazed with fiery offerings of incense. Conch shells and bone whistles sang from the towers.

NARRATOR 2: At the House of Singing, warriors drank their favorite maize porridge, perhaps for the last time. Some sang, while others danced a dance of war.

TWO FLINT: If the New Fire burned in the great temple, we would have peace. Tomorrow I will find Lord Morning Star, and tell him we need his light!

NARRATOR 1: Two Flint went to sleep, and he dreamed that the summer skies whirled their clouds around the moon.

NARRATOR 2: Lord Morning Star burst through the circle of moonlight.

MORNING STAR: Fight the nine evil ones, Two Flint. But use your wits, not your sword! I wait for you! Come! Come!

* * *

NARRATOR 1: The next morning, the mighty Aztec army, with weapons shining in the dazzling sunlight, marched away on the road to the hills.

NARRATOR 2: But on the long mountain road, a single Aztec boy set off for the Hill of the Star.

NARRATOR 1: The pale maize sun of dawn was hot amber when Two Flint came to the crossroads, where the first evil demon awaited him.

CROSSROADS: (growls) Go back! I am Crossroads, and no one passes me!

TWO FLINT: Mighty Lord Crossroads, I seek one greater than you!

CROSSROADS: Greater than I? I, who can change the path of River?

NARRATOR 2: His arms whipped up and down, faster and faster, until the banks of River shook.

NARRATOR 1: Two Flint ran to the riverbank.

TWO FLINT: Lord River! Greater than Lord Crossroads! Wash away all but the true road!

RIVER: (gurgles) I am greater than Crossroads!

NARRATOR 2: Lord River dove deep into the riverbed and filled his mouth with water. Suddenly, a giant waterspout swept away Lord Crossroads.

NARRATOR 1: Two Flint jumped past River, but water was filling the road. Two Flint's heart beat wildly.

TWO FLINT: Great Lord Wind! Mightier than Lord River! Blow Lord River back!

WIND: (howls) Wind always blows stronger than River's current!

NARRATOR 2: Over Two Flint's head a gust of wind blew, in torrents, in streams, in mighty bursts, pushing River back into his bed.

NARRATOR 1: Two Flint climbed the steep riverbank, but Lord Wind blew him down.

WIND: You fooled Crossroads and River, but you can't fool me!

TWO FLINT: I may not be powerful enough to fool you, mighty Wind, but look! Lord Storm has passed you!

NARRATOR 2: And he pointed ahead on the road to huge, gloomy black clouds. Lord Wind turned dark blue as he puffed up his cheeks and blew a giant gale. But Storm's frogs opened their mouths. Hail and rain flew like arrows across the sky, and the frogs swallowed Lord Wind.

NARRATOR 1: Two Flint's legs shook and wobbled as he scrambled up the road. Lord Storm passed behind. The ground ahead crumbled and cracked.

EARTHQUAKE: (grumbles) No one passes Earthquake!

NARRATOR 2: Two Flint grabbed the trunk of an old, gnarly tree.

TWO FLINT: If you are so powerful, why is Lord Volcano taller?

EARTHQUAKE: (grumbles then roars and shakes)

NARRATOR 1: Two Flint pressed himself tightly against the tree. The ground rippled through the tree's roots and split the bark.

TWO FLINT: Lord Volcano! Let Lord Earthquake shake the ground to pieces! You can put them back together!

NARRATOR 2: Smoke and ash filled the air. Lord Volcano poured out his fire, and the rocks melted together.

VOLCANO: (bellowing) You passed ahead of Storm and you escaped Earthquake, but you can't fool me!

NARRATOR 1: Down poured his rocky fire. Two Flint climbed from the tree to a cave high on a cliff. He held his breath as fiery rocks tumbled everywhere. When Lord Volcano stopped, the entrance was blocked. Two Flint was trapped!

NARRATOR 2: Suddenly, a cool wisp of air trickled over Two Flint's feet. He caught it in his fingers and followed it to another opening. But a shadow larger than the sky darkened the road.

SMOKING MIRROR: Go no farther! I am Lord Smoking Mirror, the great trickster, and no one passes me without first holding my cloak!

NARRATOR 1: Two Flint knew that, of all Lord Smoking Mirror's tricks, his cloak of forgetfulness was the most powerful.

NARRATOR 2: Quickly, Two Flint gathered together a pile of rocks and made a statue of himself. He pushed it out the opening. The demon swooped down, dropped his cloak over the statue, and flew away. Two Flint had tricked him!

NARRATOR 1: His heart pounding hard and loud, Two Flint ran up the road. He came to a thick mist filled with the sounds of teeth gnashing and bones clattering. Out sprang the Lord and Lady of Death, shaking their bones.

LORD DEATH: (hissing) Approach, Spirit!

LADY DEATH: (hissing) Now you belong to us!

TWO FLINT: Step back! I am still alive! I fooled seven lords. You have power over the dead, but you have no power over *me*.

NARRATOR 2: Faster than the jaguar, he shot up a steep hill and bolted through the clouds.

NARRATOR 1: Spicy incense and flowers perfumed the air. Billowy clouds sparkled brighter than all the Emperor's jewels. Two Flint was on top of the Hill of the Star.

MORNING STAR: (gently) You have struggled long and hard, Two Flint.

NARRATOR 2: High over the mist appeared Lord Morning Star, bathed in silvery rays of moonlight. Glistening gold flames encircled him.

MORNING STAR: In your search for peace, fighting with only your wits, you have found me. You are the new One of Peace, Prince Two Flint. Take the New Fire!

NARRATOR 1: A brilliant flame on a feathery torch tumbled down to Two Flint.

NARRATOR 2: Two Flint found himself running on the road toward Tenochtitlan, the New Fire glimmering in his hands. Behind him Lord Morning Star shone, spreading rays of red and gold across the sky.

NARRATOR 1: All along the walls, warriors who had fought their way into the city threw down their weapons and greeted Two Flint.

NARRATOR 2: Emperor Itzcoatl himself welcomed Two Flint as he climbed the stairs of the great temple and placed the New Fire on the altar.

TWO FLINT: Let all fighting end! From this day on, let our city be a brother to all cities!

NARRATOR 1: The people sang and danced. Itzcoatl's warriors and Tezozomoc's warriors broke their spears and embraced as friends.

NARRATOR 2: Inside the temple, the glow of a single fire burned bright and true.

The Devil and Mother Crump

By Valerie Scho Carey

Adapted from *The Devil and Mother Crump*, Harper & Row, 1987

8–10 ROLES: Narrator 1, Narrator 2, Narrator 3, Narrator 4, Mother Crump, Lucifer, Devil 1/Neighbor 1, Devil 2/Neighbor 2

10 minutes

NOTE: This story is based on a folktale common to the United States and western Europe.

NARRATOR 1: Once there was a baker woman by the name of Mother Crump. She was so stingy and mean that her husband and children ran away from home just to get shut of her.

NEIGHBOR 1: Mean as the Devil!

NARRATOR 1: . . . some folks said of her.

NEIGHBOR 2: *Meaner* than the Devil!

NARRATOR 1: . . . said others.

NARRATOR 4: Some of that talk reached clear on down to Lucifer, the very Devil himself, and it made him mighty curious. He decided to pay Mother Crump a visit, to see for himself.

NARRATOR 2: Not long after, while Mother Crump was sweeping out the bake oven, an old man knocked on her door and poked his cracked and crinkled face into her kitchen.

LUCIFER: Good woman, would you direct me to the nearest inn where I might get some food and a bed for the night?

NARRATOR 3: Mother Crump looked the old man up and down. That didn't take long, because he wasn't very tall.

NARRATOR 2: His clothes were made of rich red velvet. His eyes glowed like coals, and when Mother Crump looked into them, she saw no reflections.

NARRATOR 3: But his purse was full, and that was what mattered.

CRUMP: If you can *pay*, you're welcome to spend the night right here!

LUCIFER: I always see that those who deal with me get what they're *owed*.

* * *

NARRATOR 1: Early the next morning, when Mother Crump got up to sweep the ashes from the fire, she saw that the old man's bed was empty.

CRUMP: He's skipped out without payin'! If I ever set eyes on that good-for-nothin' again, I'll whup his hide!

NARRATOR 4: Just then, a fine-looking young man came to the door.

LUCIFER: (*sweeps hat off*) Good morning! I was hoping you might have a room I could let.

NARRATOR 1: Mother Crump looked at the young man's splendid coat and ruffled neckcloth.

NARRATOR 4: Then she looked at his eyes and saw that they glowed but held no reflections.

CRUMP: (*yanking him inside*) You! Thought you could trick me out of another night's lodging with your disguises, did you? Well, once lucky, twice a fool! Pay up!

NARRATOR 2: Mother Crump reached for her baking paddle. She swung it at Lucifer, but he skipped out of the way. Again she swung, again and again, until she had him backed up against the hearth.

NARRATOR 3: Once more she let that paddle fly, and Lucifer leaped backward, falling right smack in the ashes. A cloud of black soot spumed into the air.

NARRATOR 2: His fine clothes were ruined. His face was smeared with soot.

NARRATOR 3: Mother Crump raised that paddle to crack it down on his head.

LUCIFER: I'll pay!

CRUMP: (lowers paddle a little) Now you're talkin'!

LUCIFER: I'll give you three wishes. Anything you want!

CRUMP: I want my money!

NARRATOR 1: She swung the paddle high for another whack—but his strange, glowing eyes looked up at her, and she checked her swing.

NARRATOR 4: There was something peculiar about this fellow, she thought.

CRUMP: All right. I'll take the wishes. But I warn you, you'd better make good!

LUCIFER: I told you before! Those who deal with me get what they're owed!

CRUMP: (looking around) Let me see . . . First, I want you to make it so anyone who so much as *peeks* into my flour barrel will be clapped inside and have to stay there till *I* wish 'em out.

LUCIFER: Huh?

CRUMP: Second, I want anyone who messes with my bread dough to be stuck fast to it till *I* set 'em free.

LUCIFER: What kind of wish is that?

CRUMP: It's *my* kind. And third, anyone who dares poke around the birch tree in my yard will be tangled tight in its branches and not get free till *I* let 'em go. Agreed?

LUCIFER: If that's what you want, that's what you've got. Now help me up!

CRUMP: Help yourself!

NARRATOR 2: That was the final insult. Lucifer pulled himself up and brushed the soot from his coat.

LUCIFER: You may not know who you're talking to now, but when the time comes for you to leave this world, it's *I* who'll have the last word!

NARRATOR 3: With that, he shot straight up the chimney. But one boot caught on the bricks and flew off, giving Mother Crump just an eye-wink-full of one cloven hoof.

CRUMP: (*proudly*) Now, ain't that somethin'! That there was the Devil himself I whupped!

* * *

NARRATOR 1: Years passed, and finally the time came for Mother Crump to leave this world. Lucifer sent one of his little devils to fetch her.

NARRATOR 4: She was scooping flour from her flour barrel—the one she'd wished about—when the little devil arrived.

DEVIL 1: Let's go, Mother Crump! Lucifer is ready for you.

CRUMP: All right, all right, I'll come. But only after I get this bread baked.

DEVIL 1: Well, hurry up!

CRUMP: I'm hurrying, I'm hurrying. But, listen, if you'd reach down inside this barrel and scoop out some flour, it'd sure speed things along.

DEVIL 1: Oh, all right.

NARRATOR 1: The devil was so little, he jumped right in the barrel to get the flour.

NARRATOR 4: Mother Crump clapped on the lid.

DEVIL 1: Hey! Let me outta here!

NARRATOR 1: The little devil started rattling and thumping at the lid, but it held firm. He began leaping around inside the barrel so it pitched and swayed from side to side, till it fell right over and rolled around the kitchen.

DEVIL 1: Let me out! Let me out!

CRUMP: Do you promise to go home and leave me alone?

DEVIL 1: Yes, I'll never bother you again!

CRUMP: Sounds fair to me!

NARRATOR 4: So she took off the lid, and he lit out of there so fast, his feet never touched the ground.

* * *

NARRATOR 2: Some time later, Mother Crump was kneading her dough when she heard the clickety-clack of hooves on the wooden floor. She looked up, and there stood a second little devil, just a scratch bigger than the first.

DEVIL 2: Come on, Mother Crump! Lucifer wants me to fetch you down to Hell, and I mean to be quick about it!

CRUMP: Well, I can't go. Not till I've finished punchin' down this dough.

NARRATOR 3: And back to work she went, at a nice easy pace that just set that little devil's teeth on edge.

DEVIL 2: You're too slow! Let me in there, and I'll get this done! (*shoves her aside*)

NARRATOR 2: That little devil didn't know about Mother Crump's second wish. So he punched one fist into that dough, and it stuck fast. He punched in the *other* fist, and it stuck too! Then he stomped on the dough with his right foot, and *it* got stuck. So he stomped in with his *left* foot, and sure enough, it stuck too!

NARRATOR 3: He started to rocking back and forth, and soon he fell over and started to roll around on the floor. He rolled around and around, wrestling with that dough, till he looked like nothing more than a great lump of dough with two eyes and a tail.

CRUMP: You're doin' a fine job!

DEVIL 2: (*muffled*) Help! Gemme outta here!

CRUMP: Do you promise to go away and leave me be?

DEVIL 2: (*grunts and rocks as a nod*)

CRUMP: Then be free!

NARRATOR 2: That little devil bolted for home so fast, he left scorch marks on the path!

* * *

NARRATOR 1: Two days passed. On the morning of the third, while Mother Crump was setting her loaves in the oven, a dark shadow poured into the room, filling the place with a deep kind of darkness. Then a figure in the doorway took shape and commenced to glowing red around the edges like coals in a fire.

LUCIFER: Mother Crump! I've come to take you down to Hell!

NARRATOR 4: Lucifer's voice made her bones shiver. But Mother Crump wasn't about to give in.

CRUMP: Old goat-foot! Who do you think you are, ordering me about in my own place? I've bread to bake, so you'd best clear out, or I'll take a *birch switch* to you!

LUCIFER: Oh, you *will,* will you? Well, we'll just see who gets the whipping *this* time!

NARRATOR 1: He marched straight outside to pull a whipping switch from the birch tree. But he'd forgotten that third wish of hers. Before he could pull it down, the branches caught hold of him, scooped him up into the center of the tree, and held him fast.

NARRATOR 4: They scratched his face, tangled in his tail, and twisted around his neck so as to choke the breath out of him. The harder he thrashed, the tighter the tree held him.

LUCIFER: *(rasping and gasping)* Let me go! Get me down from here!

CRUMP: Swear that you'll go away and never bother me again, and I'll let you go!

LUCIFER: I swear it!

CRUMP: Well, then . . . be free!

NARRATOR 1: Lucifer landed with a *thump*. He picked himself up and ran off so fast, the dust didn't have a chance to kick up under his feet.

CRUMP: *(doubles over laughing)* I outsmarted *all* those devils. Now ain't I one fine lady!

*   *   *

NARRATOR 2: The years went by. Finally, Mother Crump was too old and worn out to live anymore, so she took her bread paddle and slid on down to Hell.

NARRATOR 3: When Lucifer and his little devils saw her coming, they ran to lock the gate.

LUCIFER: Get out of here! We want no more trouble with *you*, Mother Crump!

CRUMP: I won't get! I've got no place to go!

NARRATOR 2: She took her bread paddle and commenced to whacking away at the lock on the gate.

CRUMP: If you won't open up, I'll *bust* my way in.

LUCIFER: Stop! Wait!

NARRATOR 3: He reached round and picked up a red-hot coal, and shoved it through the bars at Mother Crump.

LUCIFER: Here, take this! You're just mean enough to go start a Hell of your own!

ALL: And that's exactly what she did.

How Tom Beat Captain Najork and His Hired Sportsmen

By Russell Hoban

Adapted from *How Tom Beat Captain Najork and His Hired Sportsmen*,
Atheneum, 1974

**10 ROLES: Narrator 1, Narrator 2, Tom,
Aunt Fidget Wonkham-Strong, Captain Najork, Sportsman 1,
Sportsman 2, Sportsman 3, Sportsman 4, Bundlejoy Cosysweet**

10 minutes

NOTE: Aunt Fidget Wonkham-Strong and Captain Najork are meant to be
"very British."

NARRATOR 1: Tom lived with his maiden aunt, Miss Fidget Wonkham-Strong. She wore an iron hat and took no nonsense from anyone. Where she walked, the flowers drooped. When she sang, the trees all shivered.

NARRATOR 2: Tom liked to fool around. He fooled around with sticks and stones and crumpled paper,

NARRATOR 1: with mewses and passages and dustbins,

NARRATOR 2: with bent nails and broken glass and holes in fences.

NARRATOR 1: He fooled around with mud, and stomped and squelched and slithered through it.

NARRATOR 2: He fooled around on high-up things that shook and wobbled and teetered.

NARRATOR 1: He fooled around with dropping things off bridges into rivers and fishing them out.

NARRATOR 2: He fooled around with barrels in alleys.

NARRATOR 1: When Aunt Fidget Wonkham-Strong asked,

AUNT: Tom! What are you doing?

NARRATOR 2: Tom said,

TOM: Fooling around.

AUNT: It looks very like *playing* to *me*. Too much playing is not good, and you play too much. You had better stop it and do something useful.

TOM: All right.

NARRATOR 2: But he did *not* stop. He did a little fooling around with three cigar bands and a paper clip.

NARRATOR 1: At dinner, Aunt Fidget Wonkham-Strong, wearing her iron hat, said,

AUNT: Eat your mutton and your cabbage-and-potato sog.

TOM: All right.

NARRATOR 2: He ate it.

NARRATOR 1: After dinner, Aunt Fidget Wonkham-Strong said,

AUNT: Now learn off pages 65 to 75 of the *Nautical Almanac*. That will teach you not to fool around so much.

TOM: All right.

NARRATOR 2: He learned them off.

AUNT: From now on, I shall keep an eye on you. If you do not stop fooling around, I shall send for Captain Najork and his hired sportsmen!

TOM: Who is Captain Najork?

AUNT: Captain Najork is seven feet tall, with eyes like fire, a voice like thunder, and a handlebar mustache. His trousers are always freshly pressed, his blazer is immaculate, his shoes are polished mirror-bright, and he is every inch a terror.

When Captain Najork is sent for, he comes up the river in his pedal boat, with his hired sportsmen all pedaling hard. He teaches fooling-around boys the lesson they so badly need—and it is not one they soon forget!

NARRATOR 1: Aunt Fidget Wonkham-Strong kept an eye on Tom.

NARRATOR 2: But he did not stop fooling around.

NARRATOR 1: He did low and muddy fooling around.

NARRATOR 2: He did high and wobbly fooling around.

NARRATOR 1: He fooled around with dropping things off bridges.

NARRATOR 2: And he fooled around with barrels in alleys.

AUNT: Very well.

NARRATOR 1: . . . said Aunt Fidget Wonkham-Strong, sitting at table in her iron hat.

AUNT: Eat your greasy bloaters.

NARRATOR 2: Tom ate them.

AUNT: I have warned you that I should send for Captain Najork if you did not stop fooling around. I have done that. As you like to play so much, you shall play against Captain Najork and his hired sportsmen. They play hard games, and they play them jolly hard. Prepare yourself!

TOM: All right. (*fools around some more*)

* * *

NARRATOR 1: The next day, Captain Najork came up the river, with his hired sportsmen pedaling his pedal boat.

NARRATOR 2: They came ashore smartly, carrying an immense brown-paper parcel.

NARRATOR 1: They marched into the garden.

SPORTSMAN 1: One!

SPORTSMAN 2: Two!

SPORTSMAN 3: Three!

SPORTSMAN 4: Four!

NARRATOR 2: Captain Najork was only six feet tall. His eyes were not like fire. His voice was not like thunder.

CAPTAIN: Right!

NARRATOR 1: . . . said Captain Najork.

CAPTAIN: Where *is* the sportive infant?

AUNT: *(points)* There.

NARRATOR 1: . . . said Aunt Fidget Wonkham-Strong.

TOM: *(raises hand)* Here!

NARRATOR 2: . . . said Tom.

CAPTAIN: Right! We shall play womble, muck, and sneedball—in that order.

NARRATOR 1: The hired sportsmen sniggered as they undid the immense brown-paper parcel and set up

SPORTSMAN 1: The womble run!

SPORTSMAN 2: The ladders!

SPORTSMAN 3: The net!

SPORTSMAN 4: The rakes!

SPORTSMAN 1: The stakes!

TOM: How do you play womble?

CAPTAIN: *(smirking) You'll* find out.

TOM: Who's on *my* side?

CAPTAIN: Nobody! Let's get started!

NARRATOR 2: Womble turned out to be a shaky, high-up, wobbling and teetering sort of game, and Tom was used to that kind of fooling around.

NARRATOR 1: The Captain's side raked first.

NARRATOR 2: Tom staked.

NARRATOR 1: The hired sportsmen played so hard that they wombled too fast and were shaky with the rakes.

NARRATOR 2: Tom fooled around the way he always did, and all his stakes dropped true.

NARRATOR 1: When it was Tom's turn to rake, he did not let Captain Najork and the hired sportsmen score a single rung.

NARRATOR 2: At the end of the snetch, he had won by six ladders!

CAPTAIN: (*clenching his teeth*) Right!

NARRATOR 1: . . . said Captain Najork.

CAPTAIN: Muck next. Same sides.

SPORTSMEN 1, 2, 3, & 4: (*snigger*)

NARRATOR 1: The court was laid out at low tide in the river mud.

NARRATOR 2: Tom mucked first and slithered through the marks, while the hired sportsmen poled and shoveled. Tom had fooled around with mud so much that he scored time after time.

NARRATOR 1: Captain Najork's men poled too hard and shoveled too fast, and tired themselves out.

NARRATOR 2: Tom just mucked about and fooled around. When the tide came in, he led the opposition 673 to 49!

AUNT: (*distressed*) Really!

NARRATOR 1: . . . said Aunt Fidget Wonkham-Strong to Captain Najork.

AUNT: You must make an effort to teach this boy a lesson!

CAPTAIN: Some boys learn hard.

NARRATOR 2: . . . said the Captain, chewing his mustache.

CAPTAIN: Now for sneedball!

NARRATOR 1: The hired sportsmen brought out

SPORTSMAN 2: The ramp!

SPORTSMAN 3: The slide!

SPORTSMAN 4: The barrel!

SPORTSMAN 1: The bobble!

SPORTSMAN 2: The tongs!

SPORTSMAN 3: The bar!

SPORTSMAN 4: The grapples!

NARRATOR 2: Tom saw at once that sneedball was like several kinds of fooling around he was particularly good at. Partly it was like dropping things off bridges into rivers and fishing them out, and partly it was like fooling around with barrels in alleys.

CAPTAIN: I had better tell you

NARRATOR 1: . . . said the Captain to Tom,

CAPTAIN: that I played in the Sneedball Finals, five years running.

TOM: They couldn't have been very final, if you had to keep doing it for five years!

NARRATOR 2: He motioned the Captain aside, away from Aunt Fidget Wonkham-Strong.

TOM: *(in a low voice)* Let's make this interesting.

CAPTAIN: *(also in a low voice)* What do you mean?

TOM: Let's play *for* something. Let's say, if I win, I get your pedal boat.

CAPTAIN: What do I get if *I* win? Because I am certainly going to win *this* one.

TOM: You can have Aunt Fidget Wonkham-Strong!

CAPTAIN: Hmm. She's impressive. I admit that freely. A very *impressive* lady.

TOM: She fancies you. I can tell by the way she looks at you sideways from beneath her iron hat.

CAPTAIN: No!

TOM: Yes!

CAPTAIN: And you'll *part* with her, if she'll *have* me?

TOM: It's the only sporting thing to do!

CAPTAIN: (*loudly again*) Agreed, then! (*shakes hands on it*) By George! I'm almost sorry I'll have to *teach* you a lesson by beating you at sneedball!

TOM: Let's get started!

CAPTAIN: Right!

NARRATOR 1: The hired sportsmen had first slide. Captain Najork himself barreled, and he and his men played like demons.

NARRATOR 2: But Tom tonged the bobble in the same fooling-around way he fished things out of rivers, and he quickly moved into the lead.

NARRATOR 1: Captain Najork sweated big drops, and he slid his barrel too hard, so it hit the stop and slopped over.

NARRATOR 2: But Tom just fooled around. When it was his slide, he never spilled a drop.

NARRATOR 1: Darkness fell, but they shot up flares and went on playing.

NARRATOR 2: By three o'clock in the morning, Tom had *won*—

NARRATOR 1: 85 to 10!

NARRATOR 2: As the last flare went up over the garden, Tom looked down from the ramp at the defeated Captain and his hired sportsmen.

TOM: Maybe that will teach you not to fool around with a boy who knows how to fool around!

CAPTAIN: (*starts bawling*)

NARRATOR 1: Captain Najork broke down and wept, but Aunt Fidget Wonkham-Strong put him to bed and brought him peppermint tea, and then he felt better.

NARRATOR 2: Tom took his new boat and pedaled to the next town down the river. There he advertised in the newspaper for a new aunt. When he found one he liked, he told her,

TOM: (*firmly*) No greasy bloaters, no mutton, and no cabbage-and-potato sog. No *Nautical Almanac*. And I do lots of fooling around. Those are my conditions.

BUNDLEJOY: (*giggles*)

NARRATOR 1: The new aunt's name was Bundlejoy Cosysweet.

NARRATOR 2: She had a floppy hat with flowers on it, and long, long hair.

BUNDLEJOY: That sounds fine to me! We'll have a go.

NARRATOR 1: Aunt Fidget Wonkham-Strong married Captain Najork—

NARRATOR 2: even though he *had* lost the sneedball game—

NARRATOR 1: and they were very happy together.

NARRATOR 2: She made the hired sportsmen learn off pages of the *Nautical Almanac* every night—

NARRATOR 1 & 2: after dinner.

SPORTSMEN 1, 2, 3, & 4: Yuck!

The Kid from the Commercial

By Stephen Manes

From *It's New! It's Improved! It's Terrible!*, Bantam, 1989

5 ROLES: Narrator 1, Narrator 2, Arnold, Will, Mr. Schlemp

5 minutes

WILL: *(smiling wide, gesturing toward Arnold with a pointed finger, and speaking in a TV announcer's voice)* Hey! Don't change that channel!

NARRATOR 1: Arnold was almost afraid to look, but he forced himself to turn around. All the slime that had poured out of the broken TV set was gone. It had magically changed into a boy!

NARRATOR 2: The boy was Arnold's age. He was tall and skinny and blond, and had bright blue eyes and a big smile. He was wearing a Helicopter Jones T-shirt and Helicopter Jones jeans and—of course— Helicopter Shoes.

WILL: *(spins around once and dances)*
Helicopter,
Helicopter,
Helicopter Shoes.
We're talk-ing
Helicopter,
Helicopter,
Helicopter Shoes.
(spins around again and flashes smile)

ARNOLD: You're from the commercial!

WILL: *(smiles wider)* Not just *one* commercial! Not just *two* commercials! Not merely *three*! Hey, I'm in *twenty different commercials*, each one more wonderful than the next! Isn't that *amazing*?

NARRATOR 1: Arnold was too flabbergasted to say anything.

WILL: *(holds out his hand)* You're my special friend.

NARRATOR 2: Arnold suddenly remembered—this kid had said those exact same words in last year's commercials for those ugly prune-faced dolls.

ARNOLD: *(distrustfully)* I don't even *know* you. How'd you *get* here? Where'd you *come* from?

WILL: *(does tap step and spins around)*
I come from here,
I come from there,
But I can come
From *anywhere*!

(in a low voice) Costumes sold separately.

NARRATOR 2: Arnold recognized that, too. It was the commercial for Mr. Mysterio, the amazing spy action-figure.

ARNOLD: Who *are* you?!

WILL: *(bows, still smiling)* Will Flack, at your service. Now, just tell me one thing. What exactly are we selling?

ARNOLD: *Selling?* I'm not selling *anything*. Unless maybe you're interested in a broken pair of Helicopter Shoes!

WILL: Broken? What?

NARRATOR 1: Arnold picked up his tongueless Helicopter Shoe and handed it to Will.

ARNOLD: Broken. Messed-up. Ruined.

WILL: *(brightens)* Of course! This is our never-before-offered *detachable-tongue* model! It's new! It's improved! It's—

ARNOLD: Terrible!

WILL: Terrible?

ARNOLD: Terrible.

WILL: Terrible? *That's* not terrible! Terrible is . . . (*dramatically*) Worgo, the Terrible Monstrosaur. He crushes! KRRRRRASH! He crumbles! KRRRRRRAK! He chomps! MMMMMMMUNCH! (*in his regular voice*) He's *new* from ToySel! (*in a low voice*) Batteries sold separately.

ARNOLD: (*softly*) Shhh, not so loud!

WILL: HE'S SO AMAZING, I WANT TO SHOUT IT FROM THE ROOFTOPS!

MR. SCHLEMP: (*calling*) Arnold, we've told you a thousand times!

NARRATOR 2: . . . shouted Mr. Schlemp from upstairs.

MR. SCHLEMP: *Turn down that TV set!*

ARNOLD: (*to Will*) Shhh!

MR. SCHLEMP: Arnold, did you *hear* me?

ARNOLD: (*calling back*) Sorry! I turned it down already!

MR. SCHLEMP: (*sarcastically*) *Thank* you! Good *night.*

WILL: Grouchy? *Now* there's a cure for your blues! Just—

ARNOLD: Would you stop imitating commercials for one second?! I want to know how you *got* here!

WILL: Don't be silly. *You* know why I'm here. I'm going to be in your commercial!

ARNOLD: My *commercial? What* commercial?

WILL: Stop kidding. *You* know what commercial. Any minute now we'll jump right into action. Now, what am I supposed to do? What are we selling?

ARNOLD: We're not selling *anything.* I *live* here.

WILL: *Sure* you do. At least while this *commercial's* on. (*looks around*) I know! *TV* sets! That *broken* one over there will magically turn brand-new!

ARNOLD: I wish.

WILL: No problem! All I need is the script. Or I can just make something up. Let's see. . . ."It's magic! Make your *old* TV set just like *new* with . . ." What are we selling, again?

ARNOLD: I *told* you. We're not selling *anything.*

WILL: Right! A *public service* announcement! "Lend a hand! Donate your used TV to the charity of your choice! Just phone the number on your screen."

ARNOLD: There *is* no number. There *is* no screen.

WILL: You can't fool *me.* I eat Brain Berries, the cereal that gives you the smarts!

ARNOLD: *(exasperated)* I keep *telling* you. This isn't a commercial! My TV just broke! And somehow you came through it from the inside!

WILL: *(still smiling, but suddenly worried)* Wait a minute. Your T-shirt! It doesn't *say* anything on it.

ARNOLD: So what?

WILL: It has to *say* something. Or at least have some little character on the front. It *has* to. It's a sacred rule!

ARNOLD: Maybe in *commercials.* But I keep telling you, this isn't a commercial! This is *real life.*

WILL: "Real life"? I don't know what you're *talking* about. But whatever it is, it's easy to fix. You need. . . . Now, just let me think. You need. . . .

ARNOLD: I'll *tell* you what I need! I need fast, *fast,* FAST RELIEF. But somehow—

NARRATOR 1: Arnold looked again at the shattered TV, then back at the weird kid who had come out of it.

ARNOLD: I don't think I'm going to get it.

Tapiwa's Uncle

By Nancy Farmer

Adapted from "Tapiwa's Uncle," in *Cricket: The Magazine for Children,*
February 1992

7+ ROLES: Narrator 1, Narrator 2, Tapiwa, Tongai, Father, Mother, Uncle Zeka, (Police, Firemen, House Owners)

10 minutes

NOTE: Nancy Farmer's story, originally published in *Cricket,* is now part of her first novel for American children, *Do You Know Me,* Orchard, 1992. Both story and novel are based on her experiences in Zimbabwe, where she lived and wrote for many years. *Tapiwa* is pronounced "Tah-PEE-wuh." *Tongai* is pronounced "TONG-gie" (rhymes with "pie"). *Zeka* is pronounced "ZAY-kuh."

NARRATOR 1: When Tapiwa came home from school, the police car was already in front of her house. She knew why it was there.

NARRATOR 2: Father, Mother, and her older brother Tongai were outside. She saw the man in the back seat rap on the window. Then he rattled the door handle so hard, it almost came off. Father went over quickly and opened it.

NARRATOR 1: Uncle Zeka stepped out. He was older than Father, and much thinner. Father was dressed in a business suit, because he had just come home from the bank. Uncle Zeka was dressed in baggy pants that had been mended so many times, they looked like a road map. His shirt was a grain bag, with holes cut out for his head and arms.

NARRATOR 2: Uncle Zeka looked at his new family and smiled. It was such a big, welcoming smile that Tapiwa knew she was going to like him.

NARRATOR 1: Father said politely,

FATHER: Have you eaten, my brother?

ZEKA: Yes, thank you.

NARRATOR 2: . . . said Uncle Zeka, just as politely.

ZEKA: But it is always nice to have more.

NARRATOR 1: Then Father thanked the policemen, and the family went inside. Tapiwa and Tongai sat quietly, as Mother placed dish after dish of food on the table.

NARRATOR 2: Uncle Zeka explained between mouthfuls how he had left his village in Mozambique and traveled to Zimbabwe.

ZEKA: The bandits came in the middle of the night. They had guns, and they forced everyone outside. They took everything valuable, and when they were finished, they set fire to the huts.

MOTHER: How terrible!

FATHER: You were lucky they didn't shoot you.

ZEKA: Some people were not lucky. After the bandits left, I searched the ashes of my hut, but there was nothing useful. I decided the only thing I could do was to come to you.

FATHER: Of course.

ZEKA: I walked until I crossed the border. Then I walked some more, until the police found me. After that, I got to travel in a car, all the way to Harare.

NARRATOR 1: Uncle Zeka was excited about the car, because it was the first one he had ever been in. He described how the wind had blown in his face, and how things had moved past the window. He had had to close his eyes every time they turned a corner.

NARRATOR 2: From the way Uncle Zeka talked, it sounded like nothing much had happened before the car ride. But Tapiwa knew he had walked through the bush for two weeks. Every day, he had had to hunt for water and food, without so much as a pocket knife. There were lions, leopards, elephants, and hippopotamuses in the bush, as well as many kinds of poisonous snakes.

ZEKA: Do you have a car?

FATHER: It's very old. The air conditioning doesn't work.

ZEKA: (sighs) This is a wonderful place.

* * *

NARRATOR 1: For the next few days, Tapiwa and Tongai followed their uncle around. They knew it wasn't polite to talk to an adult unless he spoke to them first, but Uncle Zeka liked to talk all the time. Tapiwa asked,

TAPIWA: What did you eat in Mozambique?

ZEKA: The same things you eat in Zimbabwe. Pumpkins, maize, fish, and caterpillars.

TAPIWA: (shocked) Caterpillars?

NARRATOR 2: Tongai hissed at her,

TONGAI: Be quiet!

NARRATOR 1: Later, when they were alone, Tongai said,

TONGAI: We mustn't make him feel different!

TAPIWA: I *know* people eat caterpillars. I've just never seen anyone *do* it!

TONGAI: Well, be careful. Father says it's going to be hard for Uncle Zeka to get used to things. He doesn't know how to use a telephone or change a light bulb. He can't read or write. He's just as smart as Father, but he never went to school.

NARRATOR 2: Most of the time, Tapiwa decided, Uncle Zeka wasn't any different from other village people who moved to the big city. He planted a vegetable garden in the back yard, and built a cage for chickens. Father bought him new clothes, and sandals because his feet were too knobbly for shoes.

NARRATOR 1: One night, when the air was still and thunder rumbled in the distance, Uncle Zeka invited Tapiwa to hunt termites with him.

NARRATOR 2: Here and there, termites were boiling out of the ground. Most of them were small and wingless, but among them were sleek, fat insects with wings.

NARRATOR 1: The fat insects were supposed to fly away and start new nests, but they didn't want to. The little termites ran around and bit them to make them go. Soon the air was full of clumsy, fluttering bodies from hundreds of nests.

ZEKA: They like light.

NARRATOR 2: . . . explained Uncle Zeka, heading for a street lamp. Thousands of termites gathered there, and he and Tapiwa scooped them into a large plastic bag. Now and then, they ate one. The termites tasted slightly sour and nutty.

NARRATOR 1: All around, frogs, toads, and lizards gathered to eat. Some of the toads were so full of food, they couldn't hop.

NARRATOR 2: Under other lights, other people stood and caught termites, but Tapiwa didn't see anyone else with a large bag.

NARRATOR 1: Back at home, Uncle Zeka rolled three rocks together in the front yard and started a fire between them. He hammered out a large tin can into a flat sheet. Then he roasted and dried the termites so they would keep.

NARRATOR 2: Later, Mother cried,

MOTHER: He ruined my flower bed! There's a burned place, right in the middle!

FATHER: He didn't know it was special. He's never raised flowers.

NARRATOR 1: A few days later, Mother found a pot cooking on the kitchen stove. It smelled terrible.

NARRATOR 2: She took off the lid to see what it was.

MOTHER: (screams)

NARRATOR 1: Inside were dozens of fat, hairy caterpillars, bobbing up and down in a kind of soup.

NARRATOR 2: Mother took a deep breath and put the lid back on. She said to Tapiwa,

MOTHER: We mustn't criticize Uncle Zeka. The people where he lived were so poor, they didn't even have chickens. They had to eat whatever they could find. I wish, though, that he would simply eat what I cook, and not try to help out!

NARRATOR 1: That night, Uncle Zeka served his caterpillar stew. But no one wanted it.

FATHER: I'm sorry. We're not used to this kind of food.

ZEKA: You're missing a good thing!

NARRATOR 2: . . . said Uncle Zeka, helping himself to a large bowlful.

NARRATOR 1: In the night, Uncle Zeka got very sick. Father had to take him to the emergency room at the hospital.

NARRATOR 2: The next day, he stayed in bed, looking gray and weak. When Tapiwa brought him tea, he said,

ZEKA: I can't understand it. They looked like the caterpillars I used to eat in Mozambique. Of course, those lived on pumpkin leaves, and these were on the death-apple tree.

TAPIWA: Oh, Uncle Zeka! They were full of poison! You might have died! Why don't you just eat what Mother cooks?

ZEKA: I want to help out!

* * *

NARRATOR 1: A few days later, Uncle Zeka announced that he wanted to hunt mice. He had an especially nice recipe for them. He took Tongai and Tapiwa to an empty lot between two houses.

ZEKA: Mice like tall grass. There are probably *hundreds* in there, fat as pigs, waiting for us to come and get them.

TONGAI: Are we going to set traps?

ZEKA: Traps?! We don't want just one or two! We're going to feed the whole family! Your father might even want to invite his boss.

TONGAI: I don't think Father's boss likes mice.

ZEKA: *Everybody* likes them! Now, the best way to collect a lot of mice is to set fire to the field.

TAPIWA: We can't do that!

TONGAI: We're too close to houses!

ZEKA: Nonsense! Grass burns so fast, it will be out before you know it.

NARRATOR 2: He gave Tapiwa a large stick, and Tongai another.

ZEKA: Tapiwa, you stand here. Tongai, you stand over there.

TAPIWA: What are we supposed to do?

ZEKA: I'll start the fire at the other end. When the mice run out, you hit them.

TAPIWA: I don't want to do that! I don't like to kill things!

TONGAI: Please stop!

NARRATOR 1: But Uncle Zeka was already at the opposite end of the field. He struck matches and walked along, setting a blaze.

NARRATOR 2: The fire shot up with a fierce, crackling sound. The flames were red, and the wind drove them toward Tapiwa and Tongai. Black smoke poured into the air.

NARRATOR 1: Above the sound of the fire came the squeaks of the mice. They poured out of the grass and ran straight for the children.

NARRATOR 2: Tongai stood hypnotized, and Tapiwa dropped her stick. The mice ran between their feet and around their legs. Then they disappeared into the gardens all around.

NARRATOR 1: A fire engine clanged its bell as it came around a corner. Men jumped off and began to beat out the fire with heavy sheets of rubber. Others ran to find water.

ZEKA: (*returning, with disappointment*) You didn't *catch* anything.

TONGAI: We've got to go!

NARRATOR 2: Tongai pulled at his uncle's sleeve, but it was already too late.

NARRATOR 1: The owners of the houses came out and grabbed Uncle Zeka. They pulled him one way and another, and shouted at him.

NARRATOR 2: Tongai ran for help.

TAPIWA: Uncle Zeka! Uncle Zeka!

*   *   *

NARRATOR 1: That night at dinner, Father said,

FATHER: You can't set fires in the city.

ZEKA: I was only trying to help out.

FATHER: I know. Your problem is, you don't like to sit idle all day. We'll have to find you a job.

ZEKA: That's an excellent idea! I know just what I can do!

FATHER: What's that?

ZEKA: Why, I can be a cook!

ALL (except ZEKA): (*gasp*)

Mr. Twit's Revenge

by Roald Dahl

Adapted from *The Twits*, Knopf, 1981

6 ROLES: Narrator 1, Narrator 2, Narrator 3, Narrator 4, Mr. Twit, Mrs. Twit

8 minutes

NOTE: For best effect, position MR. TWIT closest to NARRATORS 1 and 2, and MRS. TWIT closest to NARRATORS 3 and 4.

NARRATOR 1: Mr. Twit was a horrid old man.

NARRATOR 4: *Mrs.* Twit was no *better.* One morning, when Mr. Twit wasn't looking, she took out her glass eye and dropped it into Mr. Twit's beer.

NARRATOR 1: Mr. Twit sat slowly drinking the beer. He was trying to think up a really nasty trick he could play on his wife.

MRS. TWIT: You're plotting something!

NARRATOR 4: . . . said Mrs. Twit, keeping her back turned so he wouldn't see she had taken out her glass eye.

MRS. TWIT: You'd better be careful, because I'm watching you like a wombat!

MR. TWIT: Oh, shut up, you old hag!

NARRATOR 1: . . . said Mr. Twit. As he tipped down the last of the beer, he saw the glass eye staring at him.

MR. TWIT: *(gasps and jumps)*

MRS. TWIT: I *told* you I was watching you! I've got eyes *everywhere.* (*snickers*)

MR. TWIT: (*stares murderously at her*)

* * *

NARRATOR 2: To pay Mrs. Twit back for the glass eye in his beer, Mr. Twit slipped a frog between her bedsheets. Then he got in his own bed and waited for the fun to begin.

NARRATOR 3: Mrs. Twit climbed into bed and put out the light.

MRS. TWIT: (*screams*) There's something in my bed!

MR. TWIT: I'll bet it's that Giant Skillywiggler I saw on the floor. I tried to kill it, but it got away. It's got teeth like screwdrivers!

MRS. TWIT: Help! Save me! It's all over my feet!

MR. TWIT: It'll bite off your toes!

NARRATOR 3: Mrs. Twit fainted.

NARRATOR 2: Mr. Twit poured a jug of cold water over her head to revive her.

NARRATOR 3: When Mrs. Twit came to, the frog had just jumped on her face.

MRS. TWIT: (*screams*) Wait . . . wait a minute. That's a *frog!*

MR. TWIT: (*snickers*)

MRS. TWIT: (*stares murderously at him*)

* * *

NARRATOR 4: The next day, to pay Mr. Twit back for the frog, Mrs. Twit put some worms in her husband's plate of spaghetti.

NARRATOR 1: The worms didn't show, because everything was covered with tomato sauce and sprinkled with cheese.

MR. TWIT: Hey! My spaghetti's moving!

MRS. TWIT: It's a new kind. It's called Squiggly Spaghetti. It's delicious!

NARRATOR 4: She took a mouthful from her own plate, which of course had no worms.

NARRATOR 1: Mr. Twit started eating.

MR. TWIT: It's not as good as the ordinary kind. It's too squishy.

NARRATOR 4: Mrs. Twit waited until Mr. Twit had eaten the whole plateful.

MRS. TWIT: Do you want to know why your spaghetti was squishy?

MR. TWIT: Why?

MRS. TWIT: Because it was *worms!* (*laughs horribly*)

MR. TWIT: (*gasps and clutches throat*)

* * *

NARRATOR 2: To pay Mrs. Twit back for the worms in the spaghetti, Mr. Twit thought up a *really* clever nasty trick. One night, when the old woman was asleep, he crept out of bed and took her walking stick downstairs to his workshed. There he stuck a tiny round piece of wood, no thicker than a penny, onto the bottom of the stick.

NARRATOR 3: This made the stick longer, but the difference was so small, the next morning Mrs. Twit didn't notice it.

NARRATOR 1: Every night after that, Mr. Twit crept downstairs and added another tiny thickness of wood to the end of the walking stick. He did it very neatly, so that the extra bits looked like part of the old stick.

NARRATOR 4: Gradually, oh so gradually, Mrs. Twit's walking stick was getting longer and longer. But it was all so slow and gradual that she didn't notice how long it was getting, even when it was halfway up to her shoulder.

NARRATOR 2: One day, Mr. Twit said to her,

MR. TWIT: That stick's too long for you.

MRS. TWIT: Why, so it is! I've had a feeling there was something wrong, but I couldn't for the life of me think what it was.

MR. TWIT: There's something *wrong*, all right.

MRS. TWIT: What could have happened? It must have suddenly grown longer!

MR. TWIT: Don't be a fool! How can a walking stick grow longer? It's made of dead wood, isn't it? Dead wood can't grow!

MRS. TWIT: Then what on earth has happened?

MR. TWIT: *(grinning evilly)* It's not the *stick*, it's *you*. It's *you* that's getting *shorter*. I've been noticing it for some time!

MRS. TWIT: That's not true!

MR. TWIT: You're *shrinking*, woman!

MRS. TWIT: It's not possible!

MR. TWIT: Oh, yes it is! You're shrinking *fast*. You're shrinking *dangerously* fast. Why, you must have shrunk at least a foot in the last few days!

MRS. TWIT: Never!

MR. TWIT: Of *course* you have! Take a look at your stick, you old goat, and *see* how much you've shrunk. You've got the *shrinks*, that's what you've got! You've got the dreaded *shrinks!*

NARRATOR 3: Mrs. Twit began to feel so trembly, she had to sit down.

NARRATOR 2: But when she did, Mr. Twit pointed and shouted,

MR. TWIT: There you have it! You're sitting in your old chair, and you've shrunk so much, your feet aren't even touching the ground!

NARRATOR 4: Mrs. Twit looked down at her feet, and sure enough, the man was right!

NARRATOR 1: You see, every night, when Mr. Twit had stuck a little bit extra onto the stick, he had done the same to the legs of Mrs. Twit's chair.

MR. TWIT: Just look at you sitting in your same old chair, and you've shrunk so much, your feet are dangling in the air!

NARRATOR 4: Mrs. Twit went white with fear.

MR. TWIT: (*pointing at her*) You've got the *shrinks!* You've got them bad! You've got the most terrible case of shrinks I've ever seen!

NARRATOR 3: Mrs. Twit grew so frightened, she began to dribble.

NARRATOR 2: But Mr. Twit, still remembering the worms in his spaghetti, didn't feel sorry for her at all.

MR. TWIT: I suppose you know what *happens* to you when you get the shrinks.

MRS. TWIT: What? What happens?

MR. TWIT: Your head *shrinks* into your neck. And your neck *shrinks* into your body. And your body *shrinks* into your legs. And your legs *shrink* into your feet. And in the end, there's nothing left but a pair of shoes and a bundle of old clothes.

MRS. TWIT: I can't bear it!

MR. TWIT: It's a terrible disease. The worst in the world!

MRS. TWIT: How long have I got? How long before I end up as a bundle of old clothes and a pair of shoes?

MR. TWIT: (*solemnly*) At the rate you're going, I'd say not more than ten or eleven days.

MRS. TWIT: But isn't there *anything* we can do?

MR. TWIT: There's only one cure for the shrinks.

MRS. TWIT: Tell me! Oh, tell me quickly!

MR. TWIT: We'll have to hurry!

MRS. TWIT: I'm ready! I'll hurry! I'll do anything you say!

MR. TWIT: (*grinning*) You won't last long if you don't!

MRS. TWIT: What is it I must do?

MR. TWIT: You've got to be *s-t-r-e-t-c-h-e-d.*

* * *

NARRATOR 1: Mr. Twit led Mrs. Twit outdoors, where he had everything ready for the great stretching.

NARRATOR 4: There were one hundred balloons and lots of string.

NARRATOR 2: There was a gas cylinder for filling the balloons.

NARRATOR 3: There was an iron ring fixed into the ground.

NARRATOR 1: He pointed to it and said,

MR. TWIT: Stand here!

NARRATOR 1: He tied Mrs. Twit's ankles to the iron ring. When that was done, he began filling the balloons with gas.

NARRATOR 4: Each balloon was on a long string, and when it was filled with gas, it pulled on its string, trying to go up and up.

NARRATOR 2: Mr. Twit tied the ends of the strings to the top half of Mrs. Twit. Some he tied around her neck, some under her arms, some to her wrists, and some even to her hair.

NARRATOR 3: Soon there were fifty colored balloons floating in the air above Mrs. Twit's head.

MR. TWIT: Can you feel them stretching you?

MRS. TWIT: I can! I can! They're stretching me like mad!

NARRATOR 1: He put on another ten balloons.

NARRATOR 4: The upward pull became very strong. Mrs. Twit was quite helpless now. With her feet tied to the ground and her arms pulled upward by the balloons, she was unable to move. She was a prisoner.

NARRATOR 2: Mr. Twit had intended to go away and leave her like that for a couple of days and nights to teach her a lesson. In fact, he was just about to leave,

NARRATOR 3: when Mrs. Twit opened her big mouth and said something foolish.

MRS. TWIT: Are you sure my feet are tied properly to the ground? If those strings around my ankles break, it's goodby for me!

NARRATOR 1: And that's what gave Mr. Twit

NARRATOR 4: his *second*

NARRATOR 2: nasty

NARRATOR 3: idea.

McBroom's Fourth of July

By Sid Fleischman

Adapted from "McBroom's Fourth of July," in *McBroom's Almanac*,
Atlantic Monthly Press, 1984

4 ROLES: McBroom, Bear-Eating John, Mayor, Judge

4 minutes

NOTE: This story celebrates the "lying contest," a popular fixture of the American folklore tradition. There are several rules: All lies must be told with an absolutely straight face. The listeners must keep their faces equally straight. And no one may challenge the truth of a lie. For more, see A *Treasury of American Folklore*, edited by B. A. Botkin, Crown, 1944.

McBROOM: (*to audience*) Summertime in these parts, we get lots of lightning bugs and mosquitoes. The lightning bugs can be downright dangerous!

Take the Fourth of July. I'd gone to town for the fun and frolic, when along came Bear-Eating John. He walks on a peg leg, and has a large spider tattooed on the end of his nose. We don't see much of him, because he eats so much bear meat, he hibernates all winter. He'd come out of the woods for the fireworks, and I could see he'd brought some noisemakers of his own—a couple of sticks of dynamite in his hip pocket.

We sat on a bench with the judge and the mayor. Some folks call it the liars' bench—but there's no truth to *that*. We slapped mosquitoes and swapped stories, waiting for night to fall and the fireworks to start.

MAYOR: Bear-Eating John,

McBROOM: . . . said the mayor,

MAYOR: I can't help noticing that spider on the end of your nose. Never could. Not that it's any of our business. . . .

JOHN: I couldn't get a wink of sleep without it.

JUDGE: I don't follow you.

McBROOM: . . . said the judge.

JOHN: Well, sir, I snooze with my nose out of the blanket. That spider scares off the li-squitoes.

McBROOM: *(to John)* What in tarnation are li-squitoes?!

JOHN: Up in the woods, lightning bugs and mosquitoes have crossed. Those li-squitoes have mighty mean stingers—and their own headlights to find you at night.

McBROOM: *(to audience)* We mulled that over for a bit, for natural history is entitled to serious thought and discussion. Then *I* said,
   (to John) Bear-Eating John, have you ever *tasted* a mosquito?

JOHN: Can't say I have, McBroom.

McBROOM: Better'n frogs' legs, and a lot more meat to the bone. Last year, we had skeeters so big, you needed a barn door to swat 'em. Folks used 'em for stew meat.

MAYOR: I'll attest to that!

McBROOM: Yes, sir, fried mosquito legs are considered a delicacy, and served only on Sundays.

JUDGE: *I'll* attest to *that.*

JOHN: I declare, I didn't know your *city* mosquitoes grew so *small.* I used to *log* mosquitoes, in the *old* days.

MAYOR: Log 'em?

JOHN: For the timber! I found a place where *mountain* mosquitoes went to die. I got together a logging crew, and we hauled out the stingers. Sold 'em for telephone poles.

McBROOM: *(to audience)* Well, I couldn't let *that* pass, even though dark was falling, and swarms of lightning bugs were out, and we ought to have been moving off.
   (to John) Bear-Eating John, it's clear you've never laid eyes on a prime long-nosed *prairie* mosquito. Like the one that stung me two years ago, over in Nebraska.

JOHN: What's so unusual about *that*, McBroom?

McBROOM: I was asleep in *Iowa* at the time!
  (*to audience*) Bear-Eating John jumped to his peg leg with a jolt of surprise. That's when I noticed that the sticks of dynamite in his hip pocket were smoking and sputtering away. *Fireflies had lit the fuses!* I grabbed the sticks and heaved them clear.
  (*to others*) EVERYBODY DOWN!

(*All duck for cover, making vocal sounds of explosions.*)

McBROOM: (*to audience*) The dynamite exploded right in the middle of the waiting stock of fireworks. My, my, my! What a show!

(*Explosions finish and all get back up.*)

McBROOM: (*to audience*) Nobody got hurt, but Bear-Eating John skinned the spider tattoo off his nose. After the excitement died down, he said,

JOHN: McBroom, it near took my breath away to hear you tell about that long-nosed prairie mosquito. I imagine there are some folks who might doubt your word. Well, I'll vouch for your truthfulness. I can produce the evidence!

McBROOM: (*to John, suspiciously*) Evidence?

JOHN: I *shot down* that skeeter, McBroom. I sawed off the merest tip—

McBROOM: (*to audience*) He tapped that polished peg leg of his.

JOHN: and this is it.

McBROOM: (*to audience*) Now, that peg leg of his has a knothole in it. I'm sorry to say it, but Bear-Eating John is given to stretching the truth.

The Fools of Chelm

Jewish folktales, retold by Steve Sanfield

From *The Feather Merchants, and Other Tales of the Fools of Chelm*, Orchard, 1991

8 ROLES: Narrator 1, Narrator 2, Narrator 3, Narrator 4, Chelmite 1, Chelmite 2, Chelmite 3, Chelmite 4/Oyzar

10 minutes

NOTE: The *ch* in Chelm isn't an English *ch*, but like gargling or hawking—a *k* with the tongue not quite touching the roof of the mouth. If you can't make this sound, you can just say "Helm" or "Kelm." *Shul* rhymes with "pull." *Mikva* is pronounced "MIK-vuh."

NARRATOR 1: The town of Chelm in eastern Europe is a very special place. And Chelm is special because its *people* are special.

NARRATOR 4: They are like no others—for, you see, each and every Chelmite is a sage. They are all wise men and women.

NARRATOR 2: At least, that's what they call *themselves*. The *rest* of the world considers them fools and simpletons.

NARRATOR 3: But this does not bother the Chelmites in the least. *They* know they are the wisest people on earth, and in the end, isn't that all that matters?

NARRATOR 1: Now, the sages of Chelm enjoy nothing more than to match their wits against a good puzzle or problem.

NARRATOR 4: They thrive on the challenge of solving the most complex and knotty conundrums.

NARRATOR 2: It has been that way from the beginning—ever since they built their *shul*, or synagogue.

NARRATOR 3: The synagogue, of course, serves not only as the House of Prayer and the House of Study, but also as a town meeting place. So, naturally, it was the first structure to be built in Chelm.

NARRATOR 1: The people of Chelm were digging the shul's foundation, when a disturbing thought occurred to them.

CHELMITE 3: Wait a minute. Hold everything. What are we going to do with all this dirt we're digging up? We can't just leave it here, where we're going to have our shul!

CHELMITE 1: We never thought of that!

CHELMITE 2: What indeed are we to do with all this dirt?

NARRATOR 4: Many suggestions were made, but all were quickly rejected as unworkable.

CHELMITE 3: Wait! I have it! All we have to do is dig a deep pit. And that's where we'll shovel the dirt we're digging up for the foundation!

CHELMITE 2: Hooray!

CHELMITE 1: A genius!

NARRATOR 2: The men began to dig another pit.

CHELMITE 1: Hold it, hold it, hold it. This doesn't solve anything! What are we going to do with the dirt from *this* hole?

CHELMITE 2: Well, it's really very simple, isn't it? We'll just dig one more pit! We'll make it twice as large as this one. And that's where we'll shovel all the dirt from this hole *and* all the dirt from the foundation.

NARRATOR 3: There was no arguing with this early example of Chelmic logic, and the men returned to their work.

* * *

NARRATOR 1: No one today can be certain how many pits were dug during the building of the shul, but it is certain the shul *was* built, for the *second* public building in Chelm was the *mikva*, the ritual bathhouse.

NARRATOR 4: The Chelmites decided that the mikva should come next so that, prior to each Sabbath, holiday, or special occasion, everyone would be able to bathe correctly.

NARRATOR 2: So the sages climbed the mountains and felled some of the larger trees and rolled them down the hill.

NARRATOR 3: But when the trees were at the bottom, Dovid the Barrelmaker pointed out another problem.

CHELMITE 1: Before we carry these logs into the town, we must decide which end should be carried in first.

CHELMITE 3: What do you mean, which end?

CHELMITE 2: What difference does it make?

CHELMITE 1: What *difference?* It makes all the difference in the world! Correct me if I am mistaken, but I believe each of these logs has two ends!

CHELMITE 2: Who can argue?

CHELMITE 3: Everyone can see that each log indeed has two ends. So what?

CHELMITE 1: So it is well known that the one who goes first is the one most honored! And since we have already honored these logs by choosing them above all others to use in our mikva, we must now decide which end should be *further* honored by being carried into town first!

CHELMITE 3: That's true!

CHELMITE 2: It's a good thing we thought of it!

NARRATOR 1: Now a discussion began about which end should be so honored.

NARRATOR 4: Those who were right-handed naturally thought it should be the *right* end.

NARRATOR 2: And just as naturally, those who were *left*-handed thought it should be the *left* end.

NARRATOR 3: The debate continued through the afternoon. At last, hoping the matter might be resolved by a wisdom more penetrating than their own, they presented their problem to Oyzar the Scholar.

OYZAR: If only all problems were as simple as this, how pleasant life would be. All you need to do is cut off the left end of the log. Then you will have only *one* end, the *right* end, and that being the only end *left*, it will be the *right* end to carry into town *first*. (*leaves*)

CHELMITE 2: Brilliant!

CHELMITE 1: Remarkable!

CHELMITE 3: You can always count on a scholar!

NARRATOR 1: So Dovid brought out a saw and cut through the wood.

NARRATOR 4: A thin round fell to the ground.

CHELMITE 3: Hooray!

CHELMITE 2: Hooray, what? The log still has two ends!

CHELMITE 1: How can that be?

CHELMITE 2: Perhaps you haven't cut off enough!

NARRATOR 2: So Dovid began again.

NARRATOR 3: His saw slid back and forth until another round fell from the log.

CHELMITE 3: Hooray!

CHELMITE 2: Enough hoorays, already! There are still two ends!

NARRATOR 1: It is written that, where we truly wish to go, there our feet will carry us. Dovid was not to be put off so easily. With fierce determination, he cut round after round, until he was too weary even to lift his saw.

NARRATOR 4: Someone else took over, also cutting round after round. But no matter how many ends were cut off, two ends still remained—even though they were at last separated by less than a foot of wood.

NARRATOR 2: Foot-long logs would never do for a bathhouse. So off they went again for Oyzar the Scholar.

NARRATOR 3: When Oyzar saw for himself the tiny stub of a log, he announced,

OYZAR: There is no need to cut any more. All you have to do is carry these logs *sideways* into town. That way, both ends will be first, and both will be honored equally. *(leaves)*

CHELMITE 2: What a brain!

CHELMITE 3: What wisdom!

CHELMITE 1: That's using your noodle!

CHELMITE 2: Let's start with this long one.

CHELMITE 3: But wait!

CHELMITE 1: What now?!

CHELMITE 3: Just look at the road. It's lined with houses! These logs are too *long* to go in sideways.

CHELMITE 2: So, what's the problem? We'll simply *tear down the houses.*

NARRATOR 1: And they did.

NARRATOR 4: Of course, the houses would have to be rebuilt.

NARRATOR 2: But that would come later.

NARRATOR 3: After all, even angels can't sing two songs at once!

*   *   *

NARRATOR 1: As you might expect from such lovers of puzzles, the people of Chelm spent much time inventing and answering riddles.

NARRATOR 4: Oyzar the Scholar was a riddler of some note—though usually no one could make sense of his riddles until after they were explained.

NARRATOR 2: An example: "Why does the dog wag its tail?"

OYZAR: Because the dog is stronger than the tail! Otherwise, the *tail* would wag the *dog*.

NARRATOR 3: Another: "Why does the hair on a man's head turn gray before the hair in his beard?"

OYZAR: Because the hair on his head is at least twenty years older than the hair in his beard!

NARRATOR 1: Oyzar's own favorite was more complicated.

OYZAR: What is green and whistles and hangs on the wall?

CHELMITE 2: We give up. What is green and whistles and hangs on the wall?

OYZAR: *(chuckles)* Why, a herring!

CHELMITE 1: A *herring*? A *herring* isn't green!

OYZAR: You could *paint* it green.

CHELMITE 3: But a herring doesn't hang on the *wall*.

OYZAR: If you *wanted* to, you could hang it.

CHELMITE 2: But . . . but there's never been a herring that whistled, and there never *will* be.

OYZAR: Ha, *ha!* I just threw *that* in to make it *hard*.

*   *   *

NARRATOR 1: By now it should be clear that everyone in Chelm was steeped in the ways of wisdom.

NARRATOR 4: Yet, as wise as the Chelmites were, there were two questions they were never able to agree upon, and that remain unsettled to this day.

NARRATOR 2: The first concerns how human beings grow. Do they grow from the head *up*?

NARRATOR 3: Or do they grow from the feet *down*?

CHELMITE 3: How can you argue? When we are young, we are given our first pair of long pants, or our first long skirt. Always, these are so long, they drag on the ground.

CHELMITE 4: But as we grow, the pants or skirt keep rising until the bottoms are well above our ankles. That proves beyond a doubt that a human being grows from the feet *down*.

CHELMITE 2: No, no! It's the other way around! Just look at a line of marching soldiers. At the bottom, their feet are all on the same level.

CHELMITE 1: But when you look at their *heads*, you'll see that some are higher than others, some lower. And that shows that we grow from the head *up*.

NARRATOR 1: The other unsolved question had to do with a simple piece of bread and butter. As long as anyone could remember, it had been an accepted truth that if you drop a slice of buttered bread, it would always fall buttered side down.

NARRATOR 4: Then some of the younger sages of Chelm decided to look into the matter. When they announced their conclusion, it created an uproar.

CHELMITE 1: It's NOT TRUE that a piece of buttered bread always falls buttered side down.

CHELMITE 4: Nonsense!

CHELMITE 3: An outrage!

CHELMITE 2: To prove it, we will conduct a public scientific experiment.

NARRATOR 2: On the announced day, the town square was filled with seekers of truth. They came from miles around.

NARRATOR 3: One of the young sages held the bread, while another slowly and carefully buttered it. Then the first sage lifted the bread, with the buttered side facing the sky.

NARRATOR 1: The crowd was hushed.

NARRATOR 4: The butter began to melt.

NARRATOR 2: The sage dropped the bread.

NARRATOR 3: It fell—buttered side down.

CHELMITE 3: *Aha!* Buttered side down!

CHELMITE 4: That proves we were right all along!

CHELMITE 2: Not at all!

CHELMITE 1: It only proves that *we* buttered the *wrong side.*

* * *

NARRATOR 1: Now that you know how the people of Chelm think, and what makes them so wise, we leave *you* to answer those two unsettled questions for yourself.

NARRATOR 4: Of course, some of you might be thinking, "Why answer such questions? *I'm* no fool."

NARRATOR 2: But remember what the good folk of Chelm always say. "If you claim you are not a fool, you only show your ignorance. For is it not written that the world was delivered into the hands of fools?"

NARRATOR 3: And we ask you, is this not the world?

The Princess and the Snails

A Native American myth of the Pacific Northwest, retold by Christie Harris

Adapted from "The Princess and the Snails," in *Mouse Woman and the Vanished Princesses*, Atheneum, 1976

12+ ROLES: Narrator 1, Narrator 2, Narrator 3, Narrator 4, Mouse Woman, Stupendous-Scavenger-and-Supreme-Snail, Magnificent-Mollusca, Gigantic-Gastropod, Gorgeous-Immensity, Alai-l, Brother, Shaman, (Villagers)

16 minutes

NOTE: *Alai-l* is pronounced "Ah-LAH-ee-EL." SNAILS should speak slowly and ponderously.

NARRATOR 1: It was in the days of very long ago, when things were different. Supernatural beings roamed the vast green wildernesses of the Northwest Coast, from Alaska to California.

NARRATOR 4: One of these was Mouse Woman, the Tiny One, who could look like a mouse, or the smallest of grandmothers. Mouse Woman liked everyone and everything to be proper, so she watched the world with her big, busy mouse eyes. She especially watched the tricksters. And she watched the young people they tricked into trouble.

NARRATOR 2: A number of handsome young people had vanished mysteriously—from totem pole villages, from berry patches, and from fishing stations. Mouse Woman knew what was going on. Her big, busy mouse eyes saw everything. Her busy ears *heard* everything.

NARRATOR 3: She knew who had captured the handsome young people. She knew who now wished to capture a *princess*. And she knew who would put a stop to it all.

MOUSE WOMAN: (*to audience*) Me! *That's* who. Capture is no way to treat young people. Especially when it turns them into slaves for those insufferable Super-Snails!

* * *

NARRATOR 1: Feeding for centuries on pride and everything else in sight, the four Super-Snails had become as big as whales. They grew more and more monstrous, needing more and more slaves to gather food for their gigantic bodies.

NARRATOR 4: Like everyone else in the Place-of-Supernatural-Beings, the Super-Snails also had *human* shapes in which their spirit-selves could move around. But they had become so proud of their snail magnificence, they never *used* their human shapes—except when they needed them to trap unwary young people.

NARRATOR 2: Mouse Woman scurried into the house of the Super-Snails, the most colossal house in the Place-of-Supernatural-Beings. And there they were, as big as whales, with enormous snail shells rising above their great gray sluggishness.

NARRATOR 3: There was Stupendous-Scavenger-and-Supreme-Snail, their chief . . . his wife, Magnificent-Mollusca . . . their son, Gigantic-Gastropod . . . and the son's wife, Gorgeous-Immensity.

MOUSE WOMAN: I've come to talk to you!

NARRATOR 1: Four pairs of eyes opened to peer through the dimness of the colossal house. Four pairs of feelers moved this way and that.

STUPENDOUS: (*disdainfully*) Oh, it's *you.*

NARRATOR 1: . . . said Stupendous-Scavenger-and-Supreme-Snail.

MOUSE WOMAN: I want to talk about humans!

STUPENDOUS: Humans? Why talk about beings who have never had the good sense to take the Snail as their totem?

MAGNIFICENT: Or

NARRATOR 2: . . . said Magnificent Mollusca,

MAGNIFICENT: the good *taste* to use the beauty of a snail to decorate their canoes or their serving bowls.

GIGANTIC: Human beings are beneath our notice.

NARRATOR 3: . . . said Gigantic-Gastropod.

GORGEOUS: Except as slaves.

NARRATOR 4: . . . added Gorgeous-Immensity. Mouse Woman glared up at her. It was *she* who now wanted a *princess* to serve her.

MOUSE WOMAN: That's what I want to talk about! They shouldn't be your slaves!

MAGNIFICENT: Nonsense! They make very *good* slaves!

MOUSE WOMAN: That's not what I mean! It's bad to snatch young people away from their families!

GIGANTIC: Oh, we don't *snatch* them. They come most willingly! You know that in our human shapes our skin is as smooth and lustrous as the pearl lining of a shell. So the young people think they are eloping with the handsomest young man or woman they have ever seen.

MOUSE WOMAN: It's bad to trap them!

STUPENDOUS: *Bad?* Because it's *human?*

MOUSE WOMAN: Human?

STUPENDOUS: Certainly! When *humans* need to eat, they trap *animals*, don't they? With their snares and pits and fishnets. So, when *we* need to eat, we trap *humans*. And we don't even *eat* them!

NARRATOR 2: Things were not going as Mouse Woman had planned. Her shoulders drooped under her mouseskin blanket.

MAGNIFICENT: Also, the happiness of all snails is in our hands. And the snails grow very unhappy when humans *kick* them off the trail.

STUPENDOUS, GIGANTIC, & GORGEOUS: *(in dismay)* Oh!

MAGNIFICENT: Or, worse still, when they *step* on their beautiful, fragile little houses.

STUPENDOUS, GIGANTIC, & GORGEOUS: OH!

MAGNIFICENT: *Horrible* humans! It's our duty to *punish* them!

GIGANTIC: You will have noticed we trap only humans who have been cruel to a snail.

GORGEOUS: So we are only doing our duty to our beloved snails.

MOUSE WOMAN: I suppose it's only your duty to your beloved snails that has you scanning the countryside, just waiting for some princess to step on a little snail's house!

GIGANTIC: Of course! When a *princess* vanishes, it gets *publicity*. So there's more chance that more humans will think twice before they kick another snail off a trail—or step on it!

MOUSE WOMAN: Aren't you afraid that will do away with your supply of slaves?

GIGANTIC: Pffffffff! We'll *never* run out of thoughtless . . . careless . . . humans!

NARRATOR 3: All four Super-Snails closed their eyes in dismissal of Mouse Woman and her ridiculous ideas.

MOUSE WOMAN: You haven't heard the last of me!

MAGNIFICENT: No, I suppose that would be too much to hope.

* * *

NARRATOR 1: Now, the Place-of-Supernatural-Beings lay in a hidden valley, high on a mountain. Towering cliffs ringed the valley, and a great thorn hedge concealed it from view.

NARRATOR 4: The mountain on one side sloped down to the sea, and right at the mountain's foot lay a village. Carved cedar houses and totem poles, all brightly decorated, edged the small beach where canoes were drawn up.

NARRATOR 2: In the house of the village chief lived the princess Alai-l, who was beautiful as a wild rose. Nearly all the high-ranking young men along the coast and up the river had come to the chief and asked to marry the princess. But the chief and his wife did not fancy any of them. None was good enough for *their* daughter.

NARRATOR 3: Alai-l was becoming annoyed. She was longing to escape the village. She was getting so desperate, she even eyed her youngest brother's invention—a wooden eagle with moving parts, and thongs to make the parts move.

ALAI-L: *(impatiently)* Why can't you make that thing fly?

BROTHER: I can create it, but only the Great Eagle Spirit can make it fly. I am sending many prayers!

ALAI-L: Well, get busy!

NARRATOR 1: Alai-l walked on along the one street of the village, and just reached its end when she saw . . . a snail. Right in her pathway.

ALAI-L: *(rudely)* I suppose *you* came to marry me, *too*.

NARRATOR 4: And she kicked the snail out of the way.

ALAI-L: I've got to get out of this village!

NARRATOR 2: Alai-l headed for the beach trail. She was not supposed to leave the village without her family around her. As a princess, she carried the royal bloodline and was precious to her entire clan. But Alai-l was past caring.

NARRATOR 3: Suddenly, she came upon a young man who had been hidden by a rock.

GIGANTIC: Alai-l, my love! Come away with me!

NARRATOR 1: He was the handsomest young man Alai-l had ever seen, with skin as smooth and lustrous as the pearl lining of a shell. He held out his hand, and she took it with strange, dreamlike pleasure. Then, as if caught in a spell, she glided away with incredible speed.

NARRATOR 4: She had escaped the village by eloping with the handsomest of young men. But . . . what was happening to her? Somehow, she had no will but *his* will. She had to go where he took her. And where *was* he taking her?

NARRATOR 2: By the time they came to the colossal house in the Place-of-Supernatural-Beings, Alai-l's dreamlike pleasure had turned to nightmare.

NARRATOR 3: This was no proper village, with a proper family waiting to welcome a daughter-in-law! She glanced in alarm at the towering cliffs that walled her in.

GIGANTIC: This is where you will serve, Slave-Princess.

ALAI-L: *Slave*-Princess?

NARRATOR 1: The young man pushed her rudely into the house. In the dim light, she could see nothing at first, but only heard a big, terrible, rumbling, churning, bubbling sound. And then she made out three monstrous shapes, lying under enormous snail shells.

NARRATOR 4: With a gasp of horror, she turned to the young man. But there in his place was another monstrous shape under another enormous snail shell. It seemed to sleep, just as the other three slept, with the big, terrible, rumbling, churning, bubbling sound coming from within.

NARRATOR 2: Shuddering with horror, Alai-l cowered back into a corner. She felt a tug at her robe, and there beside her was the tiniest of old women, watching her with big, busy mouse eyes.

ALAI-L: (*softly*) Mouse Woman!

MOUSE WOMAN: Do you know where you are, Princess?

ALAI-L: No, Grandmother!

MOUSE WOMAN: You are in the house of the Super-Snails, in the Place-of-Supernatural-Beings. They captured you because you were cruel to a snail.

NARRATOR 3: Fear and remorse filled Alai-l, as she remembered the helpless, harmless snail she had kicked out of her way.

MOUSE WOMAN: Your brothers will search for you.

ALAI-L: But how will they find the way through the thorns? And how will they find the trail down the cliffs? Grandmother . . .

NARRATOR 3: But Mouse Woman had vanished.

* * *

NARRATOR 1: Back in Alai-l's village, the alarm spread swiftly. The princess had vanished! People searched the houses and the trails. But there was no sign of her.

NARRATOR 4: Then a shaman arrived from a distant village.

SHAMAN: I will find the princess.

NARRATOR 2: She put on her dancing apron that clattered with fringes of bird beaks. She put a crown of grizzly-bear claws over her long, straggly, gray hair. She picked up her medicine rattle and her white-eagle tail feather.

NARRATOR 3: Then, as the box drums throbbed through the chief's great house, she began to circle the fire in a wild leaping dance. Her dance grew wilder and faster, wilder and faster, wilder and faster—until, suddenly, she collapsed and lay as though dead.

NARRATOR 1: She lay there a long, long time, while the people waited.

NARRATOR 4: Then at last she sat up. And her eyes were the wild-glittering eyes of one who has seen things mortals do not see.

SHAMAN: I saw the Princess as my spirit-self flew about. The Super-Snails hold her captive in the Place-of-Supernatural-Beings!

VILLAGERS: (gasp)

NARRATOR 2: Alai-l's four eldest brothers each set off at once to find the Place-of-Supernatural-Beings. But one by one, as the weeks went by, they returned without success. Each had been defeated at last by an enormous, impassable hedge of thorn.

BROTHER: Now *I* will go.

NARRATOR 3: . . . announced the youngest brother.

BROTHER: And I will find my sister.

NARRATOR 1: Alai-l's brother built a fire, and threw in offerings to the Great Eagle Spirit—offerings of fat and eagle down, of red ochre and blue paint, and of the lime of burnt clamshells. Then off he went, carrying the parts of his wooden eagle.

NARRATOR 4: As though in answer to his prayers, he went straight to the cleverly-concealed opening in the great thorn hedge. He passed through, and below him stretched an awesome valley, walled on all sides by towering cliffs. Yet there were houses in the valley.

BROTHER: The Place-of-Supernatural-Beings!

NARRATOR 2: His keen eyes searched the houses and totem poles for Snail carvings.

BROTHER: There it is. That colossal house. That is where my sister is captive.

NARRATOR 3: As he waited for the cover of darkness and the faint light of starshine, he worked carefully on his wooden eagle, fitting the moving parts together and testing the thongs that moved them.

* * *

NARRATOR 1: Night fell on the Place-of-Supernatural-Beings. In the colossal house, the great, soft, slithery-slimy monsters had settled into sleep. Their big, terrible, rumbling, churning, bubbling sound filled the darkness.

NARRATOR 4: Exhausted by her labors, Alai-l huddled in her corner. Suddenly, she felt a tug at her robe.

ALAI-L: Mouse Woman!

NARRATOR 2: Another tug made her rise and follow the tiny friend-of-young-people out into the starry night.

MOUSE WOMAN: Your youngest brother is coming for you.

NARRATOR 3: Mouse Woman pointed to a spot on the top of a cliff. Alai-l caught her breath. As she watched, a mechanical eagle launched itself into the air.

ALAI-L: Oh, Great Eagle Spirit, make it fly!

NARRATOR 1: The big, jerky bird soared through the air. It was coming straight toward her! It landed close by with a splintering *thud,* and Alai-l rushed to greet her youngest brother.

ALAI-L: My dear, gifted brother! Oh, but will it ever fly *up* again?!

MOUSE WOMAN: No need! See that glisten of snail slime? That is the trail out of the valley. Hurry! Hurry!

NARRATOR 4: Alai-l and her brother were off like two deer. Their horror of what was behind them sped their feet up the glistening trail, through the hedge, and on down the mountainside.

NARRATOR 2: All night, Alai-l's brother led her swiftly along animal trails and creek beds. By morning, they were near the village. But they could hear terrible sounds behind them, as if a fire were raging through the forest.

NARRATOR 3: They raced into the village.

ALAI-L: The Snails are coming!

BROTHER: The Snails are coming!

NARRATOR 1: There was a terrible sound on the mountain, the sound of rocks rolling and trees crashing. The weight of the Snails' enormous bodies had started a landslide!

BROTHER: Everyone into the canoes!

NARRATOR 4: The canoes all shot out into deep water. From there, the horrified villagers watched the avalanche of trees and rocks and giant snail bodies bury the beautiful carved houses and crest poles. Then they watched the monsters as they slid on helplessly into the sea and sank— never to rise again.

NARRATOR 2: The Super-Snails were gone, but so was the beautiful village. A wild wailing rose from the canoes.

ALAI-L: It is a punishment from the spirits.

NARRATOR 3: . . . murmured Alai-l, remembering a little snail so thoughtlessly kicked. And a dozen more villagers remembered *many* little snails.

* * *

NARRATOR 1: Darkness had come again to the colossal house in the Place-of-Supernatural-Beings. But now there was no movement of enormous feelers. There was no big, terrible, rumbling, churning, bubbling sound coming from deep inside monstrous bodies.

NARRATOR 4: Now there was only a circle of people sitting around a fire, people whose skin was as smooth and lustrous as the pearl lining of a shell. For of course, the *spirit*-selves of the Super-Snails had not died. They had returned to take up their *human* shapes, and to lament their lost immensity.

MAGNIFICENT: (*peevishly to Gorgeous-Immensity*) You *would* have to have a *princess* to serve you.

GORGEOUS: Well, I'm sorry!

STUPENDOUS: Now, now. It's only because it *was* a princess that the tale will spread far and wide. So more people will think twice before they kick another snail out of the way.

GIGANTIC: Or step on its beautiful, fragile little house.

STUPENDOUS: I've been thinking. Now that we have to start over again with *tiny* snail bodies, perhaps I won't need to be quite so stupendous.

MAGNIFICENT: Or I quite so magnificent.

GIGANTIC: I suppose I could be a little less gigantic.

GORGEOUS: And I suppose I could be gorgeous without being such an immensity.

STUPENDOUS, MAGNIFICENT, GIGANTIC, GORGEOUS: (*sigh*)

* * *

MOUSE WOMAN: *(to audience)* It's all so strangely satisfying. The bigness of the Super-Snails brought them to smallness. And the thoughtlessness of the people made them more thoughtful. Somehow, it makes everything . . . equal! *(titters)*

Death's Dominion

By Piers Anthony

From *On a Pale Horse*, Ballantine, 1983

5 ROLES: Narrator 1, Narrator 2, Zane, Mars, Soldier

10 minutes

NOTE: *On a Pale Horse* is the first in Piers Anthony's fantasy series, Incarnations of Immortality. The other titles are *Bearing an Hourglass, With a Tangled Skein*, and *Wielding a Red Sword. Niqueldimea* is pronounced "Nickel-dime-a."

NARRATOR 1: Our story is about an unhappy young man named Zane who decides to commit suicide by shooting himself. But just as he is about to pull the trigger and blow his brains out, he sees Death coming through the door to collect his soul.

NARRATOR 2: So instead of shooting *himself*, Zane turns the gun around and shoots—and kills—Death.

NARRATOR 1: But anyone who kills Death has to take his place. And so Zane finds himself clothed in magical cloak, hood, gloves, and skull-mask, racing around the world to collect the few souls that require Death's *personal* attention.

NARRATOR 2: And along the way, of course, there's much for Zane to learn about his new job.

*   *   *

SOLDIER: Halt!

NARRATOR 1: . . . someone cried in Spanish, the translation sounding from the device in Zane's left ear. He looked around and spied a camouflaged soldier whose rifle was pointed menacingly. Zane drew his protective cloak and hood close about him.

ZANE: Where *is* this?

SOLDIER: *I'll* ask the questions! Who *are* you, and what's your business?

ZANE: I am Death, come to collect a soul.

SOLDIER: *(snaps to attention and salutes)* Oh! Yes, sir!

NARRATOR 2: The words must have come across as the recognition code for a high officer of this army. Well, if that was the way of it, Zane would play the part.

ZANE: *(curtly)* Identify yourself and your mission!

SOLDIER: Sir! I am Fernando, of the Loyal Niqueldimea Army, on patrol to rout out the Seventh Communist renegades.

NARRATOR 1: Zane remembered now. Niqueldimea was a banana republic where guerilla infiltration had been occurring for some years as the Communists sought to topple its unpopular, autocratic government. Naturally, there would be many killings here, and some would require Death's personal service.

NARRATOR 2: His countdown watch showed thirty seconds to go.

ZANE: Carry on, Fernando.

SOLDIER: *(salutes and leaves)*

NARRATOR 1: In a moment, Zane entered a rather pretty jungle clearing. But as he did so, small-arms fire erupted. A bullet bounced off his impervious cloak. There was a scream beside him, and a Niqueldimean soldier jumped up, stiffened, and spun to the ground.

NARRATOR 2: Zane needed only a glimpse before the man was buried in the brush below to see that the right side of his head was gone. He was definitely dead, but this was not Zane's client.

NARRATOR 1: More government soldiers charged into the clearing, intent on obliterating the sniper. The ground gave way under three of them and they fell, screaming, into a pit.

NARRATOR 2: Zane looked at his orientation stone. Apparently his client was in that pit.

NARRATOR 1: Zane stepped up to the edge and looked in. It wasn't pretty. It was a large, open cavity with a dozen sharpened wooden stakes set upright in the bottom.

NARRATOR 2: The three soldiers were skewered on these. Two were dead, the third dying. The third was his client.

NARRATOR 1: The soldier had somehow turned as he fell, and the cruel spike had penetrated his back and emerged from the side of his abdomen. He had been impaled excruciatingly, his head and feet dangling to the ground.

NARRATOR 2: Zane wanted to retch, but clamped his mouth shut. His hand reached down and hooked out the soldier's soul, relieving him of his agony. Then he turned away, breathing in long, shuddering efforts.

MARS: (sizing him up) You're new at this, aren't you?

NARRATOR 1: Zane turned about. A large man stood next to him. He wore brief, polished armor, a short, woven-metal skirt, and sported an ornate golden helmet, just like the picture of a Greek god of

ZANE: (in shocked surprise) War!

MARS: (mimicking) Death!

ZANE: I didn't know—

MARS: That I existed? And who but Mars, the god of war, do you suppose should supervise this altercation?

ZANE: (relaxing) No one else. I just didn't think it through.

MARS: I've been meaning to meet you. After all, we must often associate closely.

ZANE: (distastefully) Yes. I'm still breaking in. I've got the *routine* down well enough, but scenes like *this*—

MARS: This is a *good* scene. Small, but intense. It's the best that offers between major engagements.

ZANE: (repelled) You *like* your work? What's accomplished by this combat and bloodshed?!

MARS: (expansively) I'm glad you *asked* that question!

NARRATOR 2: Zane was suddenly *sorry* he'd asked it.

MARS: War is the final refuge against oppression and wrongdoing. (*points at Zane's wrist*) Your watch shows you have another client. I'll walk with you while you attend to him. (*starts off*)

NARRATOR 1: Zane saw that it was so. Now he lacked even the excuse to quit the company of this grim warrior.

NARRATOR 2: He started off after Mars.

ZANE: (*discomfitted*) What refuge do these dead *soldiers* have? How did this battle help *them?*

MARS: They have *glory! All* men must die *sometime,* and most go ignominiously, from age or illness or mishap. Only in war do large numbers get to expire in decent glory.

ZANE: *Glory?* Seems more like *gory* to *me.*

MARS: (*bellows with laughter*) Cute, Death! (*seriously again*) *You* perceive only the instant of discomfort. *I* perceive the eternal reputation! A moment of pain, for eternal fame! These men are sacrificing their blood on the altar of righteousness. This is the termination that renders their entire mundane lives sublime!

ZANE: But what about those who die fighting for the wrong cause?

MARS: There *is* no wrong cause! There are only alternate avenues to glory and honor! Surely you'll admit this is superior to what you offer *your* clients.

ZANE: (*considers, then does a take*) Your clients *are* my clients!

MARS: (*shrugging*) Your clients, my clients . . .

NARRATOR 1: They came to a ramshackle peasant house. A government soldier was passing it.

NARRATOR 2: Suddenly a child of about ten, a little girl, dashed out. The soldier swung his rifle around, but paused when he saw it wasn't a guerilla.

NARRATOR 1: The girl rushed up to him, carrying something in her hands. As she reached him, she did something to the object.

NARRATOR 2: "Hey!" the soldier yelled. "That's a grenade!"

NARRATOR 1: The girl flung her arms about him, still clutching the grenade.

NARRATOR 2: The soldier tried to get hold of it, but she clung like a leech, her thin frame possessing the strength of fanaticism.

NARRATOR 1: Then the grenade detonated.

NARRATOR 2: She had armed it as she approached.

NARRATOR 1: Pieces of the two of them sprayed outward.

NARRATOR 2: Blood splatted against the side of the house.

MARS: That was BEAUTIFUL! That child brings great honor on her family!

ZANE: *Honor?* I call it HORROR!

MARS: (*equably*) That too. They do tend to associate on such occasions. That's part of what makes even a *minor* fracas intriguing.

NARRATOR 1: Another soldier appeared. He had heard the explosion and now saw the carnage.

NARRATOR 2: This one had a hand-held flame thrower. He ignited it and swung the flame around toward the house.

NARRATOR 1: Another child, a boy, younger than the first, ran from the house toward the soldier.

NARRATOR 2: But the man played the flame thrower directly on him.

NARRATOR 1: In an instant the child was a mass of fire.

NARRATOR 2: Then the soldier focused on burning the house.

NARRATOR 1: There was a whimper from the smoking mass on the ground.

MARS: Your client, I believe.

NARRATOR 2: The Deathwatch stood at zero and pointed at the boy. Zane hurried over and took the child's soul, and the whimpering ceased.

ZANE: (*demanding*) What HONOR was there for this *child?*

MARS: Not much. He failed in his mission. Failure does not deserve reward.

ZANE: That wasn't my point! Without this *war*, there would've been no deaths at all! *I* would never have been *summoned*. All this HORROR would never have *existed*.

MARS: (*tolerantly*) On the contrary. Without this war, the oppression of this populace would have continued indefinitely, grinding the people down, dispossessing them of their property, starving them out. They would've died *later*, it's true, but in a *worse* manner—like sheep led to the slaughter. Now they're learning to die like wolves defending their territory.

ZANE: But—

MARS: Violence is but the most visible aspect of a necessary correction, much as an earthquake is a release of enormous subterranean pressures. Blame not the *symptom*, my good associate. Blame the fundamental social inequities that stifle innovation and freedom and can be corrected in no other way.

ZANE: I still don't see—

MARS: I come to right wrongs, not to wrong rights! I am the surgeon's scalpel that removes the cancer. My edge may hurt for a moment, and some blood may flow. But my cause is just—as is yours. (*walks off*)

NARRATOR 1: Zane found himself unable to refute the ready and rough-hewn logic of Mars.

NARRATOR 2: But as he looked at the still-smoking little corpse of the child whose soul he had harvested, he feared it was not God whom Mars served, so much as

ZANE: (*to audience*) The Devil.

Westwoods

By Eleanor Farjeon

Adapted from "Westwoods," in *The Little Bookroom*, Godine, 1984
(first published by Oxford, 1955)

8–13+ ROLES: Narrator 1, Narrator 2, King John, Selina, Minister 1, Minister 2, Minister 3, Princess of Eastmarshes/ (Princess of Northmountains)/(Princess of Southlands), (King of Northmountains)/(King of Southlands)/ (Hockey Player), (Citizens/Courtiers/Hockey Players)

18 minutes

NOTE: Selina is the "saucy maid," a stock figure in British theater.

JOHN: (*reading his poem, and writing the last few words*)
  I know you are sweeter than grassfields in June,
  And bright as the single star watching the moon.
  I long for my grass, and I dream of my star,
  Though I haven't the faintest idea . . . who . . . you . . . are.

NARRATOR 1: As the young King of Workaday finished writing his poem, Selina the Housemaid knocked on the door.

JOHN: (*irritated*) What is it, Selina?

SELINA: (*steps in*) Your ministers want you.

JOHN: I'm busy!

SELINA: "At once!" they said.

JOHN: Well, go tell them—

SELINA: *I've* got my *cleaning* to do.

NARRATOR 1: The King groaned and put down his pen.

SELINA: (*looking around*) While you're seeing the ministers, I could do your room, I suppose.

JOHN: Yes, but don't touch the desk, *please.* I always have to *tell* you.

SELINA: (*putting up with him*) Oh, *all* right.

NARRATOR 1: The King gave her a cross look as he started for the Stateroom.

* * *

NARRATOR 2: The Kingdom of Workaday wanted a Queen, and his ministers had come to tell the young King so.

MINISTER 1: You've come of age, Your Majesty!

MINISTER 2: It's time for you to find a wife!

MINISTER 3: And of course, she must be a princess!

JOHN: What princesses *are* there?

NARRATOR 2: . . . asked the young King, whose name was John because, as the old King his father had said, the name John had always worked well, and no nonsense about it.

NARRATOR 1: They did not believe in nonsense, there in the Kingdom of Workaday, and they kept their noses so close to their jobs that they couldn't see anything beyond them. But they did their jobs thoroughly— and it was the ministers' job to see that their King married a princess, and the King's job to marry her. So John made no fuss.

NARRATOR 2: The ministers consulted their lists.

MINISTER 1: There is the Princess of Northmountains, the country to the top of Workaday on the map.

MINISTER 2: And there is the Princess of Southlands, which lies at the bottom.

MINISTER 3: And there is the Princess of Eastmarshes, which lies on the righthand side.

JOHN: And what about Westwoods, that lies on the left?

NARRATOR 2: The ministers looked serious.

MINISTER 1: We do not *know* what lies in the West.

MINISTER 2: No one in living memory has gone there.

MINISTER 3: No one has passed the fence that stands between us and the country beyond!

JOHN: Hmm. Tomorrow I will hunt Westwoods and find out.

MINISTERS 1, 2, & 3: (*terrified*) Sire, it is *forbidden!*

JOHN: (*thoughtfully to himself*) Forbidden!

NARRATOR 1: And then John remembered how in his childhood he had been warned by his parents never to go into Westwoods.

NARRATOR 2: The mothers of Workaday had *always* warned their children of the dangers that lay beyond the fence. And no Workaday children ever lost the wish to get *into* Westwoods—until they grew up and got married and had children of their own. Then they warned their *own* children of the dangers they had never seen.

JOHN: I will hunt Westwoods tomorrow! (*starts out*)

MINISTERS 1, 2, & 3: (*gasp*)

NARRATOR 1: He went to tell Selina to put out his things, and found her leaning on her broom over his desk, reading what he had been writing.

JOHN: Don't *do* that!

SELINA: Oh, *all* right.

NARRATOR 2: She began dusting the mantelpiece. The King waited for her to say something else, but as she didn't, he had to.

JOHN: (*coldly*) I'm going hunting tomorrow. I want you to put out my things.

SELINA: Where are you hunting?

JOHN: In Westwoods.

SELINA: *(in disbelief)* Never!

JOHN: *(exasperated)* I wish you would understand that I mean what I say!

NARRATOR 1: Selina began to dust the desk, and a flick of her duster sent the King's writing to the floor. The King picked it up angrily, hesitated, and got rather pink.

JOHN: *(uncertainly)* So, you *read* this, did you?

SELINA: *(still dusting)* Um-*hm.*

JOHN: *(waits for her to say something more)* Well?

SELINA: *(stops and looks at him)* It's a bit of *poetry,* isn't it?

JOHN: *(testily)* Yes.

SELINA: I thought so. Well, I think your room's about done, now.

NARRATOR 2: And she took herself out of it. The King felt so cross with her, he crumpled his poem into a ball, and threw it in the wastepaper basket.

*   *   *

NARRATOR 1: The morrow came, and the King rode out on his white horse for Westwoods. Presently, the tall fence came in sight, and over it he jumped.

NARRATOR 2: His first feeling was of disappointment. In front of him was a barrier of brushwood. Caught in the barrier was all sorts of broken rubbish—torn pictures and broken dolls, rusty trumpets, chipped glass marbles, and useless books without covers.

NARRATOR 1: He rode through the barricade of rubbish and found a waste of flat gray sand, flat as a plate, and like a desert in size. Flat as it was, he could not see the end of it.

NARRATOR 2: The King turned his horse, rode through the barrier, and jumped to the Workaday side of the fence. Then he rode to the palace, where his ministers hailed him with joy.

MINISTER 1: Sire, you have returned!

MINISTER 2: Thank heaven you are safe!

MINISTER 3: *(anxiously)* What did you see?

JOHN: Nothing and nobody! Tomorrow I will go to Northmountains, and begin my wooing.

NARRATOR 1: And he went to his room.

JOHN: *(calling for her)* Selina! Pack my trunk!

SELINA: *(enters)* Where for?

JOHN: Northmountains, to see the Princess.

SELINA: You'll want your fur coat and your woolly gloves.

NARRATOR 2: And she went to see about them.

NARRATOR 1: The King thought his poem might come in useful too, but on looking in his wastepaper basket, he found that Selina had emptied it.

NARRATOR 2: This made him so cross that, when she brought him his glass of hot milk at bedtime, he wouldn't say "good night."

SELINA: *(indignantly)* Hmph! *(leaves)*

* * *

NARRATOR 1: The next day, the King rode to Northmountains.

NARRATOR 2: It was more than cool there, it was freezing! Some people were in the streets, but nobody so much as glanced at him.

JOHN: *(to himself)* I've never seen such stiff, cold faces in my life.

NARRATOR 1: The King rushed on to the palace, which stood upon a glacier on a mountaintop.

NARRATOR 2: The Throne Room was hung in white, and felt like a refrigerator. At the far end, the King of Northmountains sat on his throne, and his courtiers stood in rows, as stiff as statues. At the King's feet sat the Princess of the North, completely covered with a snowy veil.

NARRATOR 1: Nobody stirred or spoke. John plucked up his courage and slid across the icy floor to the King's throne.

JOHN: (*to the King*) I have come to woo your daughter.

NARRATOR 2: The King gave the slightest nod towards the Princess at his feet. John couldn't think how to begin. If only he could remember his poem! He did his best, kneeling before the silent figure.

JOHN: (*reciting loudly with no thought of the meaning*)
You're whiter than snowflakes, you're colder than ice.
I can't see your face, and perhaps it's not nice.
I don't want to marry a lady of snow.
I've come to propose, but I hope you'll say no.

NARRATOR 1: Such a complete silence followed his proposal, John began to think he must have gotten his poem wrong. He waited about five minutes, bowed, and slid backwards out of the Throne Room. When he got outside, he jumped on his horse and rode back to Workaday as fast as he could.

NARRATOR 2: His ministers were waiting impatiently.

MINISTER 1: Did all go well?

MINISTER 2: Is everything settled?

JOHN: *Quite* settled.

MINISTER 3: (*gleefully*) And when will the wedding take place?!

JOHN: Never!

NARRATOR 1: And he went to his room.

JOHN: (*shivering*) Selina! Light the fire!

NARRATOR 2: Selina was good with fires, and had a splendid one burning in a jiffy. While she was tidying the hearth, she asked,

SELINA: How did you like the Princess of the North?

JOHN: Not at all.

SELINA: Wouldn't *have* you, eh?

JOHN: (*glaring*) Learn to know your *place*, Selina!

SELINA: Oh, *all* right. Anything more?

JOHN: Yes. Unpack my bag, and pack it up again. Tomorrow, I'm going to see the Princess of Southlands.

SELINA: You'll want your straw hat and your linen pajamas.

NARRATOR 1: And she started for the door.

JOHN: Uh . . . Selina . . . um . . . do you remember how that . . . uh . . . bit of poetry of mine went?

SELINA: (*huffily*) I've got too much to do to trouble myself to learn poetry!

NARRATOR 2: She went out, and the King was so cross that, when she returned with a really hot hot-water bottle for his bed, he never said so much as "thank you."

SELINA: Hmph! (*leaves*)

* * *

NARRATOR 1: The next day, the young King set out for Southlands, and to begin with, he found the journey pleasant.

NARRATOR 2: But by the time he arrived, the sun burned so fiercely that the horse could scarcely move its limbs, and sweat poured down the King's forehead.

NARRATOR 1: The royal city was as silent as sleep, and nobody stirred in the streets. The King's horse dragged itself to the palace gates. It was as much as the King could do to stagger from his saddle and find his way to the Throne Room.

NARRATOR 2: There on a golden couch reclined the King of Southlands, with the Princess lolling on a mass of golden pillows at his feet. All around the room lounged the courtiers, on gilded couches piled high with cushions.

NARRATOR 1: The Princess *was* beautiful, thought John, only very, very fat. Her father was still fatter.

JOHN: (*to King*) I have come to woo your daughter.

NARRATOR 2: The King's smile grew a little fatter and a little drowsier. John thought he had better begin. But words and energy failed him, and he decided to recover, if he could, his lost poem. He sank on his knees before the lady.

JOHN:
You're fatter than butter, you'd melt by the fire.
You're very much fatter than I could desire.
When I see you, my courage commences to ooze.
I've come to propose, but I hope you'll refuse.

NARRATOR 1: The Princess yawned in his face. As nothing else happened, John made his way out, clambered onto his horse, and ambled back to Workaday.

JOHN: (*to himself*) I don't think that *could* have been the poem.

NARRATOR 2: The ministers were awaiting him with eagerness.

MINISTER 1: Is everything arranged?

MINISTER 2: Are you and the Princess of the South of one mind?

JOHN: (*lazily*) Entirely.

MINISTER 3: And when does she become your bride?!

JOHN: Never.

NARRATOR 1: And he went to his room.

JOHN: (*wiping sweat*) Selina! Bring me an iced orange squash!

NARRATOR 2: She made them very well, and soon had one ready for him. While he drank it, she asked,

SELINA: How did you get on with the Princess of the South?

JOHN: I didn't.

SELINA: Didn't *take* to you, eh?

JOHN: Mind your place, Selina!

SELINA: Oh, *all* right. Is that all for now?

JOHN: No. Tomorrow I am going to see the Princess of Eastmarshes.

SELINA: You'll want your raincoat and boots.

NARRATOR 1: And she picked up his bag and started to leave with it.

JOHN: Wait, Selina! Where do you put what you find in my wastepaper basket?

SELINA: It goes in the dustbin.

JOHN: Has the dustbin been emptied this week?

SELINA: I sent for the dustman specially! It seemed *extra full* of rubbish.

NARRATOR 2: Her answer vexed the King so much that, when she came in to tell him she had everything ready in the bathroom for a nice cold shower, he just drummed on the window with his back to her, as though she weren't there.

SELINA: Hmph! *(leaves)*

* * *

NARRATOR 1: The next day, on the journey to Eastmarshes, the King was met by a harsh and noisy wind that nearly blew him from his saddle. The countryside was bleak and damp.

NARRATOR 2: The city was built of gray stone without any beauty. Everyone seemed to be rushing here and there, shouting at the tops of their voices as they stamped about their business.

NARRATOR 1: As John neared the palace, the doors flew open, and a crowd of people streamed toward him. They were led by a girl with a short skirt and flying hair, carrying two hockey sticks.

PRINCESS: Can you play hockey? We're one man short! Come along!

NARRATOR 2: She thrust a stick into his hand, and he found himself dragged to a great open field behind the palace. For an hour, voices yelled in his ear, hands hurled him hither and thither, and mud spattered him from head to toe.

NARRATOR 1: At last the game ended, and the girl came over to thump him on the back.

PRINCESS: Who *are* you?

JOHN: *(weakly)* I am the King of Workaday.

PRINCESS: Oh, indeed! And what have you come for?

JOHN: To woo the Princess.

PRINCESS: You don't say! Well, go ahead!

JOHN: *(stares at her)* But . . . *you* . . . aren't. . . .

PRINCESS: Yes, I am. Why not? Go *to* it!

NARRATOR 2: John made a wild effort to muster his thoughts and get hold of his lost poem.

JOHN:
You're louder than thunder, you're harsher than salt.
We're made as we're born, so it isn't your fault.
My tastes are not yours, and your manners not mine.
I've come to propose, but I hope you'll decline.

PRINCESS: Well, I never!

NARRATOR 1: And lifting her hockey stick over her head, she made for him.

NARRATOR 2: John scrambled to his horse and put it to the gallop. At last the young King came, muddy, weary, and breathless, to his own door.

MINISTER 1: Greetings, sire!

MINISTER 2: Are you and the Princess of the East agreed?

JOHN: Absolutely!

MINISTER 3: And when will she name the happy day?!

JOHN: NEVER!

NARRATOR 1: And he rushed to his room.

JOHN: *(exhausted)* Selina! Come and turn down my bed!

NARRATOR 2: Selina was very quiet and deft about it, and soon had it looking invitingly restful and ready. As she put out his dressing gown and bedroom slippers, she asked,

SELINA: What do you think of the Princess of the East?

JOHN: I don't!

SELINA: Hadn't any *use* for you, eh?

JOHN: You forget your place, Selina!

SELINA: Oh, *all* right. Will that do, then?

JOHN: *(turns on her)* No, it won't! *Nothing* will do until I FIND MY POEM!

SELINA: Your poem? That bit of poetry, do you mean? Well, why couldn't you say so before?

NARRATOR 1: And she took it out of her pocket.

JOHN: *(exasperated)* You had it all the time!

SELINA: Why *shouldn't* I? You threw it away! *(getting angry)* And a *nice* way to treat your work! A person that can't respect his work doesn't deserve to *do* any!

JOHN: *(backing down)* I . . . I *do* respect it, Selina. I was *sorry* I crumpled it up and threw it away. I only did . . . because *you* didn't like it.

SELINA: I never said so.

JOHN: *(hopefully)* Well . . . *did* you?

SELINA: It was all right.

JOHN: *(joyfully) Was* it, Selina? Oh, Selina, I've forgotten it! Read it to me!

SELINA: That I shan't! Perhaps it'll teach you another time to *remember* what you write, before you throw it away!

JOHN: Wait! I *do* remember! Listen! *(takes her hand)*
You're nicer than honey, you're kinder than doves.
You're the one sort of person that everyone loves.
I can't live without you, I cannot say less.
I've come to propose, and I hope you'll say *yes*.

SELINA: *(looks uncomfortable, says nothing)*

JOHN: *(anxiously)* Wasn't that it?

SELINA: More or less.

JOHN: *(softly)* Selina, say yes!

SELINA: Ask me in Westwoods.

JOHN: Westwoods?! Then do *you* go to Westwoods?

SELINA: Yes, all the time! On my days off.

* * *

NARRATOR 1: The King and Selina set off for the fence that divided Workaday from Westwoods. They followed the slats of the fence, while Selina tapped each one and counted under her breath. When they came to the seven-hundred-and-seventy-seventh slat, Selina slipped her finger through a hole and tripped a little catch. The slat swung back like a narrow door, and Selina and the King squeezed through.

NARRATOR 2: The King could hardly believe his eyes. There, as before, was the barrier of branches. But the branches were living, and full of singing birds.

NARRATOR 1: It was easy to find a way through the flowers and leaves to what lay beyond, for Selina led him by the hand. Instead of a gray stretch of desert sand, the greenest of plains stretched before them, filled with gay streams and waterfalls, and groves of flowering trees.

NARRATOR 2: Everything was bathed in radiant light, like mingled sun and moonshine.

JOHN: *(wonderingly, looking at everything but her)* Oh, Selina! Why did our parents forbid us to come here?

SELINA: *(in a different, lovely voice)* Because they'd forgotten, and only knew that in Westwoods there is something that is dangerous to Workaday.

JOHN: What is it?

SELINA: Dreams!

JOHN: But why did I not see all this when I came before?

SELINA: Because you didn't bring anything or anyone *with* you.

JOHN: And this time I've brought my poem.

SELINA: (*softly*) And me.

NARRATOR 1: The King looked at Selina for the first time since they had entered Westwoods, and he saw that she was the most beautiful woman in the world.

JOHN: (*wonderingly*) Selina, are *you* a princess?

SELINA: I am, always—in Westwoods.

JOHN: (*determined*) Where is my poem, Selina?

NARRATOR 2: She gave it to him, and he read aloud,

JOHN:
I know you are sweeter than grassfields in June,
And bright as the single star watching the moon.
I long for my grass, and I dream of my star,
Though I haven't the faintest idea who you are.

   Oh, Selina . . . will you marry me?

SELINA: Yes—in Westwoods.

JOHN: (*exultantly*) And *out* of it, *too!*

NARRATOR 1: And seizing her hand, he pulled her after him, through the hedge of birds and flowers, to the other side of the fence.

JOHN: *Now*, Selina! Will you?

SELINA: (*in her usual voice*) Will I *what?*

JOHN: MARRY me, Selina!

SELINA: Oh, *all* right. (*then smiles her princess smile at him*)

NARRATOR 2: And she did.

NARRATOR 1: And on the day of the wedding, the King removed for good the seven-hundred-and-seventy-seventh slat in the fence between Workaday and Westwoods,

NARRATOR 2: so that any child—

NARRATOR 1: or *grownup*—

NARRATOR 2: could slip through,

MINISTERS 1, 2, & 3: *(happily)* forever after!

Captain Cully

By Peter S. Beagle

From *The Last Unicorn*, Viking, 1968

8+ ROLES: Narrator 1, Narrator 2, Schmendrick, Captain Cully, Jack Jingly, Molly Grue, Willie Gentle, Dick Fancy, (Outlaws)

16 minutes

NARRATOR 1: All that Schmendrick the Magician later remembered of his wild ride with the outlaws—riding, as he was, face down across a saddlebow—was the wind, the saddle's edge, and the laughter of the jingling giant who held the reins. Bushes and branches raked his face, and owls hooted in his ears.

NARRATOR 2: At last, the horses slowed to a trot, then to a walk. Sullen voices murmured somewhere ahead. Then Schmendrick's cheek felt firelight, and he looked up.

NARRATOR 1: They had halted in a small clearing where another ten or twelve men sat around a campfire, fretting and grumbling.

NARRATOR 2: A freckled, red-haired man, dressed in somewhat richer rags than the rest, strode forward and called to the giant.

CAPTAIN CULLY: Well, Jack, who is it you bring us—comrade, or captive? (*calling over his shoulder*) Add some more water to the soup, love. There's company.

JACK JINGLY: I don't know what he is, myself.

NARRATOR 1: . . . began Jack, when a thin thorn of a woman, with a pale, bony face and fierce, tawny eyes, pushed through the ring of men.

MOLLY GRUE: I'll not *have* it, Cully! The soup's no thicker than sweat, as it is! And who's this long lout?

NARRATOR 2: She inspected Schmendrick as though he were something she had found sticking to the sole of her shoes.

MOLLY GRUE: I don't like the look of him. Slit his wizard!

NARRATOR 1: She had only meant to say either "weasand" or "gizzard," but the coincidence trailed down Schmendrick's spine like wet seaweed.

NARRATOR 2: He slid off Jack Jingly's horse and swirled his cloak with both hands until it billowed feebly.

SCHMENDRICK: (to Cully) And are you truly the famous Captain Cully of the greenwood, boldest of the bold, and freest of the free?

NARRATOR 1: A few of the outlaws snickered, and the woman groaned.

MOLLY GRUE: I knew it! *Gut* him, Cully, from gills to guilt, before he *does* you, the way the *last* one did.

CAPTAIN CULLY: (bowing proudly to Schmendrick) That am I. (reciting in verse) "He who hunts me for my head shall find a fearful foe. But he who seeks me as a friend may find me friend enow." (normally again) How do you *come* here, sir?

SCHMENDRICK: On my stomach, and unintentionally—but in friendship, nonetheless. Though your leman doubts it. (nods at Molly)

MOLLY GRUE: (spits on ground in contempt)

CAPTAIN CULLY: (grins, lays arm across Molly's shoulders, then to Schmendrick) Ah, that's only the way of Molly Grue. She guards me better than I do myself. I am generous and easy, to the point of extravagance, perhaps. "An open hand to all fugitives from tyranny"—that's my motto. It is only natural that Molly should become suspicious, pinched, dour, prematurely old, even a touch tyrannical. The bright balloon needs the knot at one end, eh, Molly? But she's a good heart, a good heart.

MOLLY GRUE: (shrugging his arm off, stepping away) Hmph!

CAPTAIN CULLY: You are welcome here, sir sorcerer. Come to the fire and tell us your tale. How do they speak of me in your country? What have you heard of dashing Captain Cully and his band of freemen? (brings Schmendrick to fire)

NARRATOR 2: Actually, Schmendrick had never heard of Captain Cully before that very evening. But he had a good grounding in Anglo-Saxon folklore, and he knew the type.

SCHMENDRICK: (*warming at the fire*) I have heard that you are the friend of the helpless and the enemy of the mighty, and that you and your merry men lead a joyous life in the forest, stealing from the rich and giving to the poor. I know the tale of how you and Jack Jingly cracked one another's crowns with quarterstaves, and became blood brothers thereby. And how you saved your Molly from marriage to the rich old man her father had chosen for her. And of course, there was a certain wicked king. . . .

CAPTAIN CULLY: *Haggard*, rot and ruin him! Aye, there's not one here but's been done wrong by old King Haggard—driven from his rightful land, robbed of his rank and rents, skinned out of his patrimony. They live only for revenge—*mark* you, magician!—and one day Haggard will pay such a reckoning—

NARRATOR 1: A score of shaggy shadows hissed assent, but Molly Grue's laughter fell like hail, rattling and stinging.

MOLLY GRUE: (*mocking*) Mayhap he will. But it won't be to such chattering cravens he'll pay it. His castle rots and totters more each day, and his men are too old to stand up in armor, but he'll rule forever, for all Captain *Cully* dares.

NARRATOR 2: Schmendrick raised an eyebrow, and Cully flushed radish-red.

CAPTAIN CULLY: (*mumbling to Schmendrick*) You must understand, King Haggard has this bull—

MOLLY GRUE: (*hooting*) Ah, the Red Bull, the Red Bull! I tell you what, Cully. After all these years in the wood with you, I've come to think the bull's nothing but the pet name you give your own cowardice. If I hear that fable once more, I'll go and down old Haggard myself, and know you for a—

CAPTAIN CULLY: (*roaring at Molly*) Enough! Not before strangers!

NARRATOR 1: He tugged at his sword, and Molly opened her arms to it, still laughing. Around the fire, greasy hands twiddled dagger hilts, and longbows seemed to string themselves.

NARRATOR 2: Schmendrick spoke up, seeking to salvage Cully's sinking vanity.

SCHMENDRICK: They recite a ballad of you in my country. I forget just how it goes. . . .

CAPTAIN CULLY: (*spins to face him*) Which one?

SCHMENDRICK: (*taken aback*) I don't *know*. Is there more than one?

CAPTAIN CULLY: (*glowing*) Aye, indeed! (*calling*) Willie Gentle! Willie Gentle! Where *is* the lad?

NARRATOR 1: A skinny, lank-haired youth shambled up.

CAPTAIN CULLY: (*to Willie*) Recite one of my exploits for the gentleman. Tell the one about how you joined my band. I've not heard it since Tuesday last.

WILLIE GENTLE: (*sighs, clears throat*)
'Twas Captain Cully came riding home
From slaying of the king's gay deer,
When whom should he spy but a pale young man,
Come drooping o'er the lea?

"What news, what news, my pretty young man?
What ails ye, that ye sigh so deep?
Is it for loss of your lady fair?
Or are ye but scabbit in your greep?"

"I am not scabbit, whatever that means,
And my greep is as well as a greep may be,
But I do sigh for my lady fair,
Whom my three brothers have taken from me."

"I am Captain Cully of the sweet greenwood,
And the men at my call are fierce and free.
If I do rescue your lady fair,
What service will ye render me?"

"If ye do rescue my lady fair,
I'll break your nose, you silly old gowk.
But she wore an emerald at her throat,
Which my three brothers *also* took."

Then the captain has gone to the three bold thieves,
And he's made his sword to shiver and sing.
"Ye may keep the lass, but I'll have the stone,
For it's fit for the crown of a royal king."

Then it's three cloaks off, and it's three swords out,
And it's three swords whistling like the tea.
"By the faith of my body," says Captain Cully,
"You now shall have neither the stone nor she."
(continues reciting in mime)

NARRATOR 2: Captain Cully rocked and hummed and parried three swords with his forearm for the remaining seventeen stanzas of the song, rapturously oblivious to Molly's mockery and the restlessness of his men. At last, the ballad ended.

SCHMENDRICK: Very nice. Wonderful.

CAPTAIN CULLY: Good Willie, good boy, now recite the others. *(beaming at Schmendrick)* I said that there were several ballads about me. There are thirty-one, to be exact, though none are in the Child collection, just at present. *(suddenly getting excited)* You wouldn't be Mr. Child himself, would you? He often goes seeking ballads—so I've heard—disguised as a plain man. . . .

SCHMENDRICK: No. I'm very sorry. Really.

CAPTAIN CULLY: *(droops and sighs)* It doesn't matter. One always *hopes,* of course, even now—to be collected, to be verified, annotated, to have variant versions, even to have one's authenticity doubted. . . . Well, well, never mind. *(to Willie)* Recite the other ballads, Willie lad. You'll need the practice, one day, when you're field-recorded.

NARRATOR 1: The outlaws grumbled and scuffed, kicking at stones. A voice bawled from a safe shadow,

DICK FANCY: Nah, Willie, tell us a *true* ballad. Tell us one about Robin Hood!

CAPTAIN CULLY: *(instantly on guard)* Who *said* that?

NARRATOR 2: Cully's loosened sword clacked in its sheath as he turned from side to side. His face suddenly seemed as pale and weary as a used lemon drop.

MOLLY GRUE: *I* did. The men are bored with ballads of your bravery, captain, darling. Even if you *did* write them all yourself!

CAPTAIN CULLY: *(winces)* Molly! *(looks sidelong at Schmendrick and in a low, worried voice to him)* They can *still* be folk ballads, can't they, Mr. Child? After all—

SCHMENDRICK: I'm not Mr. Child. Really, I'm not.

CAPTAIN CULLY: I mean, you can't leave epic events to the *people.* They get everything wrong!

NARRATOR 1: An aging rogue in tattered velvet slunk forward.

DICK FANCY: Captain, if we're to have ballads—and I suppose we must— then we feel they ought to be true ballads about real outlaws, not this lying life *we* live. No offense, captain, but we're really not very merry, when all's said—

CAPTAIN CULLY: *(coldly)* I am merry twenty-four hours a day, Dick Fancy. That is a fact!

DICK FANCY: And we don't steal from the rich and give to the poor. We steal from the *poor,* because they can't fight back, most of them. And the *rich* take from *us,* because they could wipe us out in a day.

We don't rob the fat, greedy Mayor on the highway. We pay him tribute every month to leave us alone! We never carry off proud bishops and keep them prisoner in the wood, feasting and entertaining them, because Molly hasn't any good dishes—and besides, we just wouldn't be very stimulating company for a bishop.

When we go to the fair in disguise, we never win at the archery or at singlestick. We *do* get some nice compliments on our disguises—but no more than that.

MOLLY GRUE: *(quietly remembering)* I sent a tapestry to the *judging,* once. It came in fourth. Fifth. It showed a knight at vigil. Everyone was doing vigils, that year. *(starts crying softly)*

NARRATOR 2: Suddenly she was scrubbing her eyes with horny knuckles.

MOLLY GRUE: (*softly but bitterly*) Damn you, Cully.

CAPTAIN CULLY: (*in exasperation*) What! What! Is it *my* fault you didn't keep up with your weaving? Once you had your *man*, you let all your accomplishments go! You don't sew or sing anymore, you haven't illuminated a manuscript in years—and what happened to that viola da gamba I got you?

DICK FANCY: (*breaking in*) And as for righting wrongs and fighting for civil liberties, that sort of thing, it wouldn't be so bad—I mean, I'm not the crusader type myself, some are and some aren't—but then we have to listen to those ballads about wearing Lincoln green and aiding the oppressed. We *don't*, Cully. We turn them in for the reward, and those ballads are just embarrassing, and there's the truth of it.

NARRATOR 1: Captain Cully ignored the outlaws' snarls of agreement.

CAPTAIN CULLY: (*with folded arms*) Recite the ballads, Willie.

WILLIE GENTLE: I'll not! And you never fought my brothers for any stone, Cully! You wrote them a letter, which you didn't sign—

NARRATOR 2: Cully drew back his arm, and blades blinked among the men as though someone had blown on a heap of coals.

SCHMENDRICK: (*steps forward with forced smile*) If I may offer an alternative, why not let your guest earn his night's lodging by amusing you? I am no hand at ballads, but I have my own accomplishments, and you may not have seen their like.

JACK JINGLY: Aye, Cully, a magician! 'Twould be a rare treat for the lads.

NARRATOR 1: The men shouted with quick delight, and the only reluctance was shown by Captain Cully himself.

CAPTAIN CULLY: (*protesting sadly*) Yes, but the *ballads*. Mr. Child must hear the *ballads*.

SCHMENDRICK: And so I *will*. Later.

NARRATOR 2: Cully brightened then, and called to his men,

CAPTAIN CULLY: Give way! Make room!

NARRATOR 1: They sprawled and squatted in the shadows, watching with sprung grins as Schmendrick began to run through the old flummeries with which he had entertained the country folk at the Midnight Carnival. It was paltry magic, but he thought it diverting enough for such a crew as Cully's.

NARRATOR 2: But he had judged them too easily. They applauded his rings and scarves, his ears full of goldfish and aces, with a proper politeness but without wonder. Offering no true magic, he drew no magic back from them. And when a spell failed, he was clapped just as kindly and vacantly as though he had succeeded.

NARRATOR 1: Cully smiled impatiently, and Jack Jingly dozed, but it startled the magician to see the disappointment in Molly Grue's restless eyes.

NARRATOR 2: Sudden anger made him laugh. He dropped seven spinning balls that had been glowing brighter and brighter as he juggled them, let go all his hated skills, and closed his eyes. He muttered to the magic,

SCHMENDRICK: Do what you will. Do what you will.

NARRATOR 1: It sighed through him then, beginning somewhere secret— in his shoulderblade, perhaps, or in the marrow of his shinbone.

NARRATOR 2: Then his heart filled and tautened like a sail, and something moved more surely in his body than *he* ever had. It spoke with his voice, commanding.

SCHMENDRICK: (*loudly, swaying, with eyes closed*)
Legends old are never done.
Shadows shrink before the sun.

NARRATOR 1: Weak with power, Schmendrick sank to his knees and waited to be Schmendrick again. He had done *something,* but he had no idea what it was.

NARRATOR 2: He opened his eyes. Most of the outlaws were chuckling and tapping their temples, glad of the chance to mock him. Captain Cully had risen, anxious to pronounce that part of the entertainment ended.

MOLLY GRUE: *(in a soft, shaky voice)* Look!

(All turn to look and remain frozen in awe.)

NARRATOR 1: A man came walking into the clearing. He was dressed in green, but for a brown jerkin and a slanting brown cap with a woodcock's feather in it. He was very tall, too tall for a living man. The great bow slung over his shoulder looked as long as Jack Jingly, and his arrows would have made spears or staves for Captain Cully.

NARRATOR 2: Taking no notice at all of the still, shabby forms by the fire, he strode through the night and vanished, with no sound of breath or footfall.

NARRATOR 1: After him came others—one at a time, or two together—some conversing, many laughing, but none making any sound.

NARRATOR 2: All carried longbows and all wore green, save one who came clad in scarlet to his toes, and another gowned in a friar's brown habit, his enormous belly contained by a rope belt. One played a lute and sang silently as he walked.

NARRATOR 1: The bowmen moved across the clearing, effortlessly proud, graceful as giraffes—even the tallest among them, a kind-eyed giant.

NARRATOR 2: Last of all came a man and a woman, hand in hand. Their faces were as beautiful as though they had never known fear.

MOLLY GRUE: *(softly, in awe)* Oh. Marian.

CAPTAIN CULLY: *(nervously)* Robin Hood is a *myth*, a classic example of the heroic folk figures synthesized out of need. Men have to have heroes, but no man can ever be as big as the need—and so a legend grows around a grain of truth, like a pearl. *(grudgingly)* Not that it isn't a remarkable *trick*, of course.

NARRATOR 1: All but the last two figures had passed into the darkness, when Dick Fancy cried out.

DICK FANCY: Robin! Robin! Mr. Hood, sir! Wait for me! *(rushes off)*

WILLIE GENTLE: And for me! Robin! Marian! Wait! *(rushes off)*

NARRATOR 2: The man and the woman had passed from sight, but every man of Cully's band, save only Jack Jingly and the captain himself, rose and ran off to the clearing's edge—tripping and trampling one another—then went crashing into the woods after the shining archers.

CAPTAIN CULLY: *(calling after them)* Fools! Fools and children! It was a *lie*, like all magic! There is no such person as Robin Hood!

MOLLY GRUE: *(softly)* Nay, Cully, you have it backward. There's no such person as you, or me, or any of *us*. Robin and Marian are real, and *we* are the lie. *(calling)* Wait! *Wait!*

NARRATOR 1: She ran on like the others, leaving Captain Cully and Jack Jingly to stand in the trampled firelight and listen to the magician's soft laughter.

Appendix: From Story to Script

Stories on Stage may provide more scripts than you'll ever need. Still, I hope you and your young readers will create some of your own. It's great fun to take a favorite story, adapt it, then be in it!

Almost any story can be presented in reader's theater, but some are easier and work better than others. In general, look for stories that are simple and lively, with lots of dialogue or action, and with not too many scenes or characters.

SCRIPT ROLES

First study your chosen story to identify the roles. There are two basic types: *Narrators* tell the story. *Characters* are *in* the story. (In first-person stories, of course, the narrator is also a character.) To help your readers understand the types, you can explain that character parts appear in the story *inside* quotation marks, while narrator parts appear *outside*.

If the group you're working with is small, a story may have more roles than you have readers. In some such cases, a story may simply not be practical for you. But there are often ways to adjust:

- Assign individual readers more than one role. But make sure a reader isn't onstage with more than one role at a time!
- "Cut" a character, or combine it with another. Speeches of one character can often be added to those of another.
- Use *character narration* in place of a separate narrator. With this approach, characters read the narrator parts that refer to them or reflect their point of view. This takes some getting used to, though, and often feels clumsy and unnatural.

Instead of too few readers, you may have more than you need. Here are some ways to involve more of them:

- Use two or more narrators. This is usually a good idea anyway for young readers. See below for tips on splitting narration.
- Split characters into two or more. A character can sometimes be converted into a set of characters, with the speaking parts divided among them.

- Assign silent characters. Often stories have minor characters without speaking parts. If your directing style includes stage movement, you can assign these roles to surplus readers. You might also add speeches for them. Crowd scenes can always use extra readers.

CUTS AND CHANGES

Feel free to make cuts and changes in the story that will make your script livelier, simpler to understand, or easier to perform. But be sure to read through and check whether everything in the story still makes sense.

Some authorities on reader's theater object to even the most minor changes in the author's work. But the author was not writing for performance. If you refrain from making appropriate changes, the author's work may not appear in its best light.

Here are some things you may want to "cut":

- Tag lines. These are the lines that tell us "he said" or "she said." In performance, these seldom do more than break up the flow of the story and trip up the readers. But leave in the ones that give extra information the audience must hear. Also leave in ones that an author has used to build rhythm.
- Long descriptions. Many stories include long sections of narration that slow the action. These can often be shortened or even removed.
- Minor characters or scenes. Cutting these can simplify the stage action and/or adjust for a small number of readers. Often, important dialogue or information can be shifted to another character or scene.

Here are other areas where you might make changes:

- Character splitting or combining. As mentioned earlier, you can combine two or more similar characters into one, or split one into two or more.
- Additional speeches. Some story characters may have no lines, or may be onstage for a long time before they speak. In these cases, you may want to invent brief speeches for them. Also, if the narration tells *about* what a character said, you might convert this into a speech of the character.
- Stage directions. You can often make the script smoother by converting parts of the narration to stage directions for the characters.
- Difficult or obscure language. Though readers should be encouraged to read "up" from their level, some scripts will be much easier to follow—for both readers and audience—if you now and then substitute a simpler word, or split a sentence in two. With foreign stories, you may want to "translate" unfamiliar terms.

- Sexist or demeaning language. Often this can be changed unobtrusively. If not, the story may not be appropriate for young people.
- Aids to reading. You can underline or italicize words that should be stressed, add commas to delineate phrasing, or insert stage directions to indicate the feeling behind speeches.

NARRATION

In scripts for younger readers, it's usually best to have two or more narrators. Besides creating extra roles, it spreads the responsibility for this very important function. It also helps retain audience interest during long narrative passages.

Splitting the narration can be done as simply or as artfully as you like. The way that is best often depends on how the story was written. Here are some possibilities:

- Assign alternate paragraphs and/or half-paragraphs. It is best to adjust the splits so Narrator 1 begins each new scene. This limits the reassignments made necessary by later script changes, such as adding or removing a single narrator speech.
- Assign alternate scenes.
- "Bounce" back and forth between narrators in a way that reflects an author's strong rhythmic structure. This can mean trading off on sentences, or even on phrases.
- "Sandwich" the dialogue. One narrator speaks both before and after a section of character dialogue. Then another narrator does the same.
- Assign a narrator to each character. Each narrator reads all the lines that refer to their assigned character or that reflect their character's point of view.
- Share the narration with the characters themselves. This form of character narration works best if the characters don't actually mention themselves.

SCRIPT FORMAT

Scripts should be neat and easy to read. Readers are supposed to look up often from their scripts, and they will have trouble finding their place again if the page is too crammed with text—*or* if the text is too spread out.

I recommend the following format:

- 12-point type. On a typewriter or in a character-based word processor, this is known as pica type, which produces 10 characters per inch. (Elite type, at 12 characters per inch, is also common on typewriters, but is too small.)

- Linespacing set at 1½ (halfway between single spacing and double spacing).
- Left margin, 1½ inches—extra-wide for binding and to let readers add stage directions. Right margin, 1 inch. Top margin, 1 inch, including the header. Bottom margin, ½ inch or more.
- Right-hand header with one or two key words from script title, plus page number.
- Block paragraph format—no regular or hanging paragraph indent. Two Returns (one blank line) after each speech.
- Ragged right (no right-margin justification).
- No speeches (or at least paragraphs) split between one page and the next. Your word processor may let you "protect" a paragraph or marked block against splitting, or let you "keep lines together." If not, you can insert a hard page break above the speech.

TEAM SCRIPTING

Children working in teams are easily capable of scripting short, simple stories. Here is one approach:

First explain briefly about identifying types of roles, adjusting for more or fewer readers, and possible cutting. Divide the readers into teams of about four. Assign a one-page story to each team, with each member receiving a copy. (Fables work well.)

The team members read through their story, identify the roles, and divide the roles among themselves. Then they decide who will read what. Each reader underlines his or her own speaking parts—in pencil, to allow changes—and also crosses out anything the whole team agrees to cut. These individual copies can later be compiled into a master script in standard format.

Normally, young readers can have a one-page story ready for tryout in about a quarter hour, with practically no adult help. *With* adult help, it can take quite a bit longer.

Resources

Books

The following books offer additional scripts and techniques:

Bauer, Caroline Feller. *Presenting Reader's Theater: Plays and Poems to Read Aloud.* Bronx: H. W. Wilson, 1987. Primary grades.

Coger, Leslie Irene, and Melvin R. White. *Readers Theatre Handbook: A Dramatic Approach to Literature.* 3rd ed. Glenview, Ill.: Scott, Foresman, 1982. College.

Latrobe, Kathy Howard, et. al. *Readers Theatre for Young Adults: Scripts and Script Development.* Englewood, Col.: Libraries Unlimited, 1989.

———. *Social Studies Readers Theatre for Young Adults: Scripts and Script Development.* Englewood, Col.: Libraries Unlimited, 1991.

Laughlin, Mildred Knight, et. al. *Readers Theatre for Children: Scripts and Script Development.* Englewood, Col.: Libraries Unlimited, 1989.

———. *Social Studies Readers Theatre for Children: Scripts and Script Development.* Englewood, Col.: Libraries Unlimited, 1990.

Pickering, Jerry V. *Reader's Theatre.* Encino, Cal.: Dickinson, 1975. College.

Sloyer, Shirlee. *Readers Theatre: Story Dramatization in the Classroom.* Urbana, Ill.: National Council of Teachers of English, 1982. Elementary.

Organizations

Readers Theatre Script Service
P.O. Box 178333
San Diego, CA 92177
619–276–1948
Individual scripts for all ages.

Institute for Readers Theatre
P.O. Box 17193
San Diego, CA 92177
619–276–1948
In-services and workshops.

Chamber Readers
P.O. Box 2013
McKinleyville, CA 95521
Performances and workshops.